By the same author

PROSE
Two in a Boat: A Marital Rite of Passage

POETRY
Parables & Faxes
Zero Gravity
Keeping Mum
Chaotic Angels
Sonedau Redsa a Cherddi Eraill
Cyfrif Un ac Un yn Dri
Y Llofrudd Iaith
Tair Mewn Un

Sunbathing in the Rain

A CHEERFUL BOOK
ABOUT
DEPRESSION

Gwyneth Lewis

HARPER PERENNIAL
London, New York, Toronto and Sydney

Harper Perennial
An imprint of HarperCollins*Publishers*
77–85 Fulham Palace Road,
Hammersmith
London w6 8jb

www.harperperennial.co.uk

This edition published by Harper Perennial 2006
6

First published in Great Britain by Flamingo in 2002

PS™ is a trademark of HarperCollins*Publishers* Ltd

A catalogue record for this book
is available from the British Library

ISBN-13 978-0-00-723280-2
ISBN-10 0-00-723280-2

Aquatint and drypoint etching by Goya entitled 'Que Se La Llevaron'
courtesy of Index/Bridgeman Art Library

Printed and bound in Great Britain by
Clays Ltd, St Ives plc

To anybody who suffers from depression:
'DO NOT BE DISCOURAGED.'

CONTENTS

INTRODUCTION

Every serious episode of depression is a murder mystery. Your old self is gone and in its place is a ghost that is unable to feel any pleasure in food, conversation or in any of your usual forms of entertainment. You become a body bag. Moving a pile of books can take days, as the objects in a room have a stronger will than your own. You are both the corpse and the detective. Without alibis – work, a social life – there's nowhere to go. Your job is to find out which part of you has died and why it had to be killed.

I gave in to my most recent bout of depression when I started driving to work one day and found that I couldn't stop crying. I thought this was odd and drove home in order to re-do my make-up before going in to the office. I went to bed and slept almost continuously for two weeks. It was five weeks before I could read again and I was off work for eleven months in all. It was two years before I began to feel like myself again.

My first impulse was to hide my condition from even my closest friends. I felt ashamed of my wretchedness, as if I'd brought it on myself. Depression's sepia light feels like despair but isn't. I'm not a wimp, a moaner nor a quitter, and normally I love my life. After all, what did I have to feel bad about? I was happily married to Leighton, had a good job, was fit and my poetry was doing well. I'd been sober for nearly ten years. I told myself that feeling bad under the circumstances amounted to ingratitude.

When I finally started to tell people what had been wrong with me I was astonished to find that I hadn't fooled anybody. Furthermore, it seemed that everybody had either experienced depression themselves or had watched someone close to them suffering.

The statistics are striking. According to the World Health Organisation, a hundred million new cases of depression are reported every year. It seems ironic that, as our standard of living improves, our capacity to enjoy it is jeopardised. As the world becomes smaller, a terrifying internal desert is opening inside us. The terrain is largely unmapped and dangerous, claiming many victims through suicide.

The connection between artistic activity and mental illness has already been well documented. In terms of the statistics, writing poetry could be classed as a dangerous occupation, like coal mining or deep-sea diving. Dylan Thomas described being a poet as 'walking on your eyeballs'. But to my mind, writing is more likely to be part of the answer to despair than its cause. Not writing is much worse! When I first met the Australian poet Les Murray, who has written his own book on the black dog, he suddenly turned to me and asked 'Do you suffer from depression?' I was very taken aback, as I was then perfectly well and hadn't mentioned the disease.

'Ha!' he exclaimed, when I confessed that I did. 'I told you I could see round corners!'

Later, I asked Les what was the cure for depression. He didn't hesitate: 'The truth'. We are all the artists of our own lives. We shape them, as best we can, using our experience and intuition as guides. But we're also natural liars and we get things wrong. It's so easy for the internal commentary that forms how we live to become a forgery. Approached in a certain way, depression is a lie detector of last resort. By knocking you out for a while, it allows you to ditch the out-of-date ideas by which you've been living and to grasp a more accurate description of the terrain. It doesn't have to come to this, of course, and most people are able to discern their own truths perfectly well without needing to be pushed by an illness. But my imagination is strong and it takes some people longer than others to sort out pleasing fancies from delusions.

If you can cope with the internal nuclear winter of depression and come through it without committing suicide – the disease's most serious side effect – then, in my experience, depression can be a great friend. It says: the way you've been living is unbearable, it's not for you. And it teaches you slowly how to live in a way that suits you infinitely better. If you don't listen, of course, it comes back and knocks you out even harder the next time, until you get the point.

Over twenty years I've discovered that my depression isn't a random chemical event but has an emotional logic which makes it a very accurate guide for me. It kicks in when I'm not listening to what I really know, when I'm being wilful

Sunbathing in the Rain

and harming myself. Much as I hate going through it, I've learned that depression is an important gift, an early warning system I ignore at my peril. I'm aware, however, that there are many degrees of depression and that everybody experiences the disease differently. In this book I'm talking not about catastrophic events in the blood chemistry but about the kind of depression which seems to be a combination of genetic inheritance, emotional habit and stressful life events. I consider myself to be at the luxury end of the depression market because I'm able to use it as a psychic white stick, knowing that it will take me to safety. I can even trust it, ultimately, to improve the quality of my life. This knowledge is no easy optimism but has been hard won through bitter experience. If this kind of depression is a gift it is, indeed, a dark one.

The story I tell in these pages will be my own personal whodunnit. I offer it only as an example of how it's possible to come through depression and profit from it, while my memory of it is still fresh. I have no desire to prolong or dwell on the experience for a second longer than necessary. Now that I'm well again, I want to get on with my life and the last thing I need is to live in the memory of such misery. I'd go so far as to say that writing a book about depression as you're coming out of a serious episode is not to be recommended because there's too much reliving involved. My main motive in writing *Sunbathing in the Rain* is the hope that it might offer some comfort and encouragement to others going through this agonising and perplexing experience.

I am by no means a confessional writer. Writing helps me

to understand my life, but it's not a cheap form of therapy. In this book I've talked more openly than I would normally about myself because depression is a powerful enemy and it thrives on secrecy. Telling my version of events has been a struggle for me even in writing *Sunbathing in the Rain* because sticking to my own point of view, in the face of strong competing stories, has always been one of my difficulties.

There are, of course, other people involved in this story. I've confined myself to those events which are relevant only to the murder mystery posed by my last bout of depression. However, it's one thing to be searingly honest about one's self and quite another to be gratuitously revelatory about others. Throughout this book I've taken great care to write only what happened factually and how it affected me. The people involved will, I know, have their own vigorous and legitimate points of view.

I'm particularly grateful to my mother for taking my account of her depression in good part. She is well known as an outstanding teacher of English, an achievement only made the greater by her long and private struggle with depression. I hope that the people who know us will only think the more of her, as I do, for all the difficult things I have to say about the effect of her suffering on me.

The feelings you experience during a bout of depression appear melodramatic and out of touch with reality to those who are not ill. People who have been through real depression will know that I'm not exaggerating in these pages. I'd even go so far as to say that depressed and non-depressed are mutually exclusive orders of perception. The brain chemistry involved bears me out on this. Both ways of seeing seem as if they are on the same emotional scale, ranging from normal despondency to desolation. This, however, is a trick of the light. Once you have passed from one state to the other, you might as well have crossed the river Lethe, whose waters make it impossible to remember the life you've left for the underworld. In depression the whole personality has crashed, leaving you as exposed as a chick in the Arctic. You have no resources to fend for yourself in high emotional winds, facing the inevitable frostbite.

But there are things you can do to help yourself. These are seldom mentioned in self-help books because the very concept of 'self-help' has missed the point. The last thing you need as a depressive is any of your own bright ideas because they are what got you into trouble in the first place. Looking back, I can see that the way I was living just before I crashed was driving me nuts, except that I couldn't recognise this.

In the middle of my illness I looked for a book to help me get through its agony. It needed to have short passages because I couldn't concentrate for long. Following a recipe was too much for me. Anything 'medical' was out. Some writers have argued, interestingly, that the persistence of depression in modern man shows that the disease offers an ongoing evolutionary advantage to society as a whole. This is nice to know for the human race, but does nothing to help the sufferer. Such books might explain the physical causes of depression, but I needed to know how to get from minute to minute without giving up. Exhortations to 'take some physical exercise' were useless when I couldn't even put on my earrings. What I wanted was accounts of experience from the front line, along with suggestions of how to survive. I needed a human perspective, practical hints and, most important of all, reassurances that I could come through my hell, that I wouldn't be caught in that existential no-man's-land forever.

Sunbathing in the Rain is my attempt to write the book I was looking for while I was recovering from depression. It draws on diaries which I kept (when I could write at all), quotes from my reading, stories I saw in the papers, anecdotes – anything that shed light on or gave me relief from feeling so wretched. The impact of my crash shattered my life, like a windscreen. It took some time to put it back together, but the exercise forced me to look at the individual pieces and decide if I wanted to return them to the picture.

I've mentioned that I'm a poet. Fiddling with words has always been the most natural way for me to respond to life, as it gives me an added perspective on my problems, a view which is wider than my own. Your 'poetry' might be fishing, dowsing or growing bonsai trees – anything that opens you to inspiration and those important insights which seem to come to you 'for free' when you're thinking about something else.

Aside from my marriage, writing poetry is the best thing in my life. I do, however, have a responsibility for the maintenance of that gift and depression may be one of the mechanisms that shows me when I'm not doing what I should. Sometimes it feels as though depression is my system cracking the whip creatively, a spur I've learned to take very seriously.

I am hoping that writing this book will be a kind of exorcism for me, proving that I have learnt what my depression taught me well enough so that I won't have to go through it again. I'm very aware that writing about depression is like trying to nail down fog, but that never stopped a writer from trying. What I'd really like to achieve is a cheerful book about depression.

Sunbathing in the Rain is aimed primarily at those who are depressed at the moment and who are looking for something nourishing to read as they go through their terrors and recover. I've structured the book like a jigsaw puzzle. Each piece should make sense on its own, but you can read them as clues to the puzzle because the whole thing adds up to a story. If you're ill, this book is designed to be read as quickly or as slowly as you need. You're in charge of the pace. It's also aimed at those who aren't ill themselves but who are watching someone close to them struggling. Depressed people are a pain, however much you love them. The best thing you can do is to keep them company, try to keep cheerful yourself and allow the patient to be unwell for as long as it takes. I can't praise enough how Leighton supported me. He fed me, never reproached me for being ill and, most importantly, never told me to get a grip.

In order to come through this last episode of depression, I had to take a view on how the self works. This was a practical matter and became a principle of survival. You don't have to share this model of the mind, which is drawn from Zen Buddhism, in order to make use of it in a crisis. The important thing is that it helps. I've included quite a few quotations from religious sources in this book because, even if you have no spiritual faith, the Church has always described the psychology of mental disorder vividly and given practical advice about how to handle it. I urge atheists and agnostics to take the valuable insights offered by these writers and not to be put off by the theological language in which they're couched. It may be no accident that the huge increase in the incidence of depression seems to have gone hand in hand with the decline of religion in the West and the loss of a whole tradition hugely experienced in dealing with failure, dejection and the sense of meaninglessness. It looks as though we might soon be able to call the early years of the twenty-first century the Age of Depression.

Depression is a serious disease and should never be taken lightly. I can't stress too much how important it is to go to your doctor. I took the anti-depressants prescribed and am very grateful for the emotional space they gave me while I gathered my resources. Anyone who looks down on people who accept this kind of help just hasn't suffered enough to know any better. I was very fortunate in that my GP, Dr Parsons of the Minster Road Practice in Cardiff, recognised my depression instantly and treated it wisely and carefully throughout. I'm grateful for his firmness and common sense.

I owe an even greater debt to Dr Richard Scorer, Consult-ant Psychiatrist of Sully Hospital, near Cardiff. I could not have hoped to have a better experience of long-term psychi-atric care than my time with him over the last decade. Dr Scorer's perceptiveness, generosity and commitment have made a huge difference to what's been possible in my life. I also want to thank him for reading this manuscript, a task well beyond the call of duty, especially as he'd already heard most of it several times before.

I also need to thank Rowan Williams for his time and wisdom over the years and Sister Elaine McInness for her guidance. My colleagues at the BBC were kinder to me than they needed to be and I'd like to give special thanks to Geraint Talfan Davies. I owe the idea of emotional 'hooks' to Michelle of the Chameleon Beauty Clinic. Malcolm Guite gave valuable feedback and I'm grateful for his perspicacity. My debt to my husband, Leighton, is clear from nearly every page of *Sunbathing in the Rain*. He truly is a diamond on a cushion.

But the most important thing to know is this: depression doesn't last forever. No matter how bad you feel, you can survive and come out into the sunlight on the other side.

Sunbathing in
the Rain

CHAPTER ONE

Day for Night

I didn't know that, when I was sleeping, Leighton would come up to the bedroom to check if I was still breathing. He's not a cry-baby, but he told me much later that he wept because he was convinced I was dying.

Under the duvet, an internal ice age had set in. I had permafrost around my heart. This is what dying of cold must be like, once the numbness has started. Outside, on the landing, two decorators were papering the hall. I slept through their radio, chat, everything. I couldn't have cared less if the house had caught fire around me. I didn't even try to lift my head off the pillow. I felt mildly surprised when Leighton brought me tea, which he never does, but I couldn't get round to drinking it so that, too, went cold.

It was as if I was pinned down by an irresistible wind. I curled up like a frozen prawn. Although I wasn't cold objectively, I acted as though I was desperately trying to conserve my body heat. Leighton would come into bed at night, as if he were slipping into my sleeping bag to keep me warm, cuddling me while the blizzard which had cut me off from the rest of the world raged on inside me. The only thing that gave me any comfort was the feel of his hand on my back.

I was down to zero visibility. My gas supply was running dangerously low and oxygen starvation made my thinking sluggish. I was aware of sheer drops on either side of my path, so I moved carefully from bed to bathroom, in case I slipped and lost my way entirely.

There was radio silence from my dreams. I am usually an inventive dreamer but now that my ordinary life was over, I suppose that my subconscious had lost its daily raw materials of anecdote and fantasy, and had nothing to report.

Leighton once told me a horrific story.

During the war, his family acquired a monkey. Its previous owner was a breeder of Alsatians but the monkey soon wore out its welcome because of its habit of hanging from the balls of his prize Alsatian. The monkey was bad-tempered and created havoc in the black-market transport café which Leighton's mother ran in their Cardiff kitchen, so they passed him on to a group of Waafs billeted next door.

The Waafs in the house grew to hate the pet because it ate their lipstick and pulled their hair. One day a group of them caught the monkey and put it on top of a barrage balloon that had landed nearby. Soon the monkey was floating at roof level.

A few hours later, the poor monkey was found on the partially deflated balloon, frozen to death.

I can't bear to think of the creature's terror, shifting between freezing and trying to keep its balance on its precarious planet. It could see the whole sky, had everywhere to jump and yet nowhere to go.

I have no head for heights. I know the loneliness of that creature on a globe that could no longer support him. He defeated his first enemy, height, but couldn't fight the cold. He became his own memorial statue.

What happened? Who killed me?

In less than a week, I'd gone from being a person who cared about clothes, being out in the world, writing, food, to being a wreck who cowered from everything. I couldn't read the books I started before my assassination. Like a corpse, my hair and nails continued to grow. Peristalsis had stopped.

I looked down at my body. A dressing-gowned lump kept following me around but seemed largely unrelated to me.

In a rare moment of animation I screamed at Leighton 'I *need* drugs!' I knew I wouldn't survive without them this time. We went to the doctor the following morning. He handed me a sick note and I asked him what I should do with it. My first death certificate.

*

Altitude Sickness

> **hypoxia, aerospace**, also called altitude sickness, a
> condition in which the body is starved of oxygen
> because of the thinness of the air at high altitudes . . .
>
> The pilot's responsibility while flying a plane is
> to remain alert and functioning. Hypoxia affects
> both these capabilities. Up to around 9,000 feet
> (about 2,750 metres) there may be headaches, respir-
> atory changes, sleepiness, difficulty in concentrating,
> and indifference. Night vision becomes less keen at
> this level, and the pilot may have a feeling of alco-
> holic intoxication. Memory can also be impaired.
>
> **The New Encyclopaedia Britannica**, 15th Edition,
> Micropaedia, Vol V, p. 259

If, instead of deflating, the barrage balloon had continued to
rise, carrying the unfortunate monkey on its crest, eventually
the creature's blood would have begun to boil at body tem-
perature.

But, long before that, the monkey had more pressing problems to face. If it had been of a philosophic turn of mind,
it might have considered that, bad as it was, its present plight
was no more than an extreme version of its true existential
condition. We all face death alone and even the most elabor-
ate religious structure is likely to be left far behind, like
scaffolding, on the last vertiginous journey into infinity. The
monkey would have been quite right to feel depressed, under
the circumstances, fully entitled to tell anybody who urged
it to be cheerful where to shove their optimism.

This is depressive realism. It has been documented that
depressive people have a more accurate conception than do

optimists of their abilities and their limits. The depressive possesses a clarity which can't be clouded by comforting lies. It may be that strenuous 'positive thinking' has a beneficial effect on the immune system and your earning capacity but what's the point of being well if it's based on an illusion? Besides, such aerobics of the morale are exhausting.

Your positive thinker may do well in suburbia but I'd rather be with a lucid depressive in the Arctic, where survival depends on precision and not fooling yourself about your chances on the ice.

> Wildlife organisations are investigating why growing numbers of Britain's swans are dying as they mistake rain-soaked roads for rivers and crash-land on them.
>
> Conservationists believe one of the wettest winters on record may be to blame for an increase of up to 25% in the number of swans injured or killed in this way . . .
>
> Swans, weighing about 8kg (18lb), come in to land with their feet outstretched, expecting a gentle touch-down. Instead they crash to a halt, leading to sprains, cut feet, injured backs and wings, and broken legs. Many injured birds are then run over and killed.
>
> Edin Hamzic and Guy Dennis, *Sunday Times*,
> 4 March, 2001

*

I could hardly remember where I was. From being able to recall what I ate and wore on most occasions in my life, including the names of everybody's aunties, I couldn't remember a thing. Not what I did half an hour ago, not the English word for 'kettle', nor whether I'd taken my pills.

This amnesia was a mercy. It made me an unreliable witness against myself, but that didn't matter because it was far too early to begin the murder enquiry anyway. I felt as though I'd taken in too much, was a piece of film that had been double- and triple-exposed. What I needed was less information, not more.

As I got used to this new limitation, I started to enjoy it. It forced me to live in the present. It was like throwing ballast out of a balloon. Once you start, why not get rid of everything? I had no use for phone numbers now – I couldn't even talk. Lightness might be better than knowledge; a view better than a parachute.

So you're dug into your duvet snow-shelter and you're not going to die of exposure just yet. Above you, it's white-out. Tumults of air are tussling and writhing so you hunker down, frightened by the din.

The crucial thing here is not to listen to your mind. What's going on there is: 'Shit! I'm in trouble, I knew it would always come to this, there's nowhere to go, no rest. This is terrible.

They're bound to sack me, if only I hadn't . . . Why can't I get up? Get up! I can't. I must get up and climb a mountain then bake a cake then go to the gym, that would show them that I'm OK. Everyone else is fine; it's only me who's mad. I've lost it. This is the end of me. Oh my God, I can't bear this . . .'

Your best bet is to keep very close to the ground, don't raise your head an inch into the wind. Expose yourself to this onslaught and you're lost, even though it is your own mind that has created this gale, what Les Murray calls a 'head-storm'. Stay still and even these enormous, terrifying powers will pass.

It's like this: your mind has got its basic communication lines crossed. If you try to fly in this flak you will shoot down your own aircraft. Friendly fire is just as fatal as being killed by the enemy. In this case, you *are* the enemy. Keep close to yourself, as if you were in a trench, fly under your own radar. Let the anti-aircraft guns discharge their ammunition into the plaid sky. Steal home, undetected even by yourself.

Whatever you do, in this state, *don't think*.

Bad day. All I could do was breathe and sleep.

*

People who are prone to depression will do almost anything to avoid feeling it. Drinking alcohol, which is a depressant, is a particularly poor form of evasive action, though I gave that one a good try. Working too much is less easy to detect as a problem because it looks like virtue and accords with the Protestant Work Ethic.

If you'd asked me a week before my collapse, I'd have told you that I'd never felt better. I'd just finished writing my fifth book of poems and was being trusted with a good deal of responsibility at work. I'd started learning to meditate and was well into practising Zen competitively. I was physically fit and could run on a treadmill for thirty minutes, a feat of which I was very proud. When my sister saw me running in the gym she collapsed laughing: 'I've never even seen you run before!'

But slightly odd things kept on happening. For example, I was sent to a big conference of the BBC's top managers in London. At lunchtime I saw someone who looked vaguely familiar and asked a colleague 'Who's that?' It turned out I'd been sitting opposite him all morning. My colleague asked, with concern in his voice, 'Is this turning out to be a long day for you?' I went to another meeting at which some mind games were being played, dressed up to the nines in my navy pinstripe suit. I noticed the woman who was chairing glance at my feet. Instead of socks I'd put on a pair of thick stockings that morning. They'd fallen round my ankles, over my boots, like wrinkled elephant skin. It did rather spoil the effect of the Jaeger suit.

My friends Deryn and Michael came down to Cardiff for

the launch of Deryn's new book of poetry. As we were sitting in the house having coffee after the reading, we heard a police helicopter hovering above us. I rushed outside, very excited, and stood in the helicopter's searchlight at the door of our house. There were shadowy figures in an unmarked police car on the corner. I wanted them to come and arrest me, wanted to be interrogated in strong lamplight – anything to be free of the unease I'd been trying to avoid feeling for months. Standing in that floodlight, looking up was like being caught by the eye of God, in a golden pillar. I nearly put my arms up so that I could be lifted away. I would have gone willingly and confessed to anything.

decompression chamber, small, airtight room in which excessive air pressure can be gradually reduced to atmospheric pressure; it is used by deep-sea divers and others, such as caisson or tunnel workers, who labour under high pressure to return to normal pressure conditions slowly. Rapid change from high pressure to atmospheric pressure can cause decompression sickness, commonly called bends, that may result in paralysis or death.

The New Encyclopaedia Britannica, 15th Edition,
Micropaedia, Vol III, p 426

*

Depression's not always about being forced down. It's more about coping with sudden changes in atmospheric pressure.

I know exactly when the internal switch in my blood flicked me into depression. Busy as usual at the week end, I'd given a poetry reading in west Wales, had visited friends on their farm and then gone out to dinner. The following morning, I woke up and knew I had no more running in me. I was in big trouble. I was floating, blood singing in my ears and an unaccustomed silence in the head.

In the blink of an eyelid I'd moved from intense self-imposed pressure to a much lighter poundage per square inch, like an astronaut reaching weightlessness, moving from 3-g to nothing in a moment. The shock had given me a dose of the emotional bends.

Imagine feeling sick, not only in your stomach but throughout your body – your arms, your cheeks, even the palms of your hands, a bit like sea-sickness but the more virulent for being less physical. It's as if your brain is trying to vomit a toxin out of itself, but it never gets the satisfaction of a good purge. It's dry retching through all your nerves, shedding none of the poison it wants to excrete, because your neural body is a closed system.

Back in Cardiff, in the week following my coming home from work, I slept up to twenty-three hours a day. In my duvet pressure-chamber, the weight dropped off me as I tried frantically to adjust to this new rate of gravity. And failed.

*

What the mind needs is weights, not wings.

Henry James

I'm using words now to try and describe the most lethargic part of being depressed, but I had gone entirely beyond words.

I found even listening to other people oppressive and would drift off in the middle of sentences. Leighton always comes back to the house having seen someone or heard some gossip, but even his stories, which I usually love, left me cold and I instantly forgot them. In previous illnesses I've found great comfort in listening to the radio in bed, sleeping through the chat of human voices, as if I were a baby in the womb – within reach of conversation but not required to take part in it. This time I couldn't bear any such noise because the disturbance inside me was so overwhelming that it took all my energy to ride it out.

I could talk to friends who phoned to see how I was only for a few minutes. However pleased I was to hear from them, soon my voice went flat and I wanted to go back to sleep. It was beyond me how other people could talk so much.

*

I didn't cry again after the first episode in the car, but I felt as if there were something stuck in my throat. Try as I might, I couldn't shift the aching, which was tight, like grief, in my larynx.

A friend told me later that her boyfriend, when he was depressed, was so convinced that he had an obstruction in his throat that he asked to be referred to a specialist. The body's a literalist and I must have taken on something too big to swallow in one go. Whatever it was, I couldn't digest it, but it had gone too far for me to spit it out. This was the first clue about what had brought me to this state, a Sleeping Beauty with the poisoned apple lodged in her gullet. What I needed was a prince to jolt the glass coffin. Or a lot more gastric juices!

1. That which is digested wholly, and part of which is assimilated and part is rejected is – Food.
2. That which is digested wholly – and the whole of which is partly assimilated, and partly not, is – Medicine.
3. That which is digested, but not assimilable, is – Poison.
4. That which is neither digested, nor assimilated is – mere obstruction.   Coleridge, *Table Talk*

*

If we hadn't turned the mattress from time to time, you'd have been able to see a clear impression of my body pressed on it. During those first weeks I lay so still that I felt like I'd become a funerary statue on my own tomb.

I did move occasionally, but this took huge effort. Everything had stopped flowing inside me, was stuck. It seemed to take hours to pick up a towel and get into the shower. Even then I saw myself as a series of statues, not a moving entity.

Instead of a film I was a series of stills: my hands up in the shower, me bent down to wash my legs, holding the soap like a prayer, then back in bed again, looking at the wallpaper. This wasn't live action but like being a model in a stop-frame animation film. Changing every stance was time-consuming and laborious but didn't seem to add up to a plot, a life.

The first day I got up it took me all morning to get showered and dressed. Once that was done I was so tired that I had to go back to bed. I settled, like a dog, on Leighton's side, in order to be near to his smell.

I was being eaten alive by time.

In normal life you're able to tune in and out of the present at will, as when you're driving and can't remember the last few miles of motorway. The slowing down of the psycho-motor functions is a classic symptom of depression. Internally it felt as though the rate of time had decreased to an unendurable pace.

I'd watch, incredulous, as putting cereal into a bowl took forever. Sitting downstairs became a marathon of endurance because there was no escape from the dullness of each second, which had stretched so that it seemed like hours. I had no way of screening out boredom, so it made me scream internally. The ordinary afternoon light refused to change, it was going to stay like that all day and I'd never be able to move again and God why couldn't it do something instead of just continuing?

It's difficult to describe how oppressive this sense of time can be. A night shirt that had fallen outside the dirty clothes-basket would irritate me intensely and I'd look at it for hours, hating it and yet totally unable to do anything about it. I felt like a ghost in my own life. Together these two sensations made being conscious a torture.

If I'd had the energy, I would have wrecked the room, just to prove that I hadn't become invisible. As it was, I just closed my eyes on it and felt sick when I opened them, a few seconds or aeons later, and still the light on that damned night shirt hadn't changed a bit.

*

Hungry spirits can see human food from a distance
but, when they approach it, it disappears like a
mirage and they have to experience the anguish of
disappointment . . .

Hungry spirits also experience special sufferings
because of their peculiar shape. Their throats are
blocked so that even when they obtain food they
can swallow it only with great difficulty . . . When
they try to move about their legs can hardly support
their bodies.

Geshe Kelsang Gyatso,
Joyful Path of Good Fortune,
(Tharpa Publications, London, 1990), pp. 187–88

The last thing I expected a Zen master to offer me was
Indulgence ice cream.

'I don't know why I'm here', I'd told Sister Elaine, a few
years earlier. She'd made us a cup of tea and we were sitting
in her Oxford flat. Driving up from Cardiff, I'd thought that,
if I was lucky, she'd offer me a cup of tea which was sure to
be beige and wan, as I imagined nuns to be. I was wrong.
The tea, when it came, was Arizona-tan, strong enough to
give you a good shot of caffeine. 'Tea's got to help you stand
up,' she said and I warmed to her.

By the time I left, she had agreed to take me on as her
student. I feel strongly that meditation should only be undertaken with a qualified and responsible teacher. I was brought
up Methodist and, at that time, wasn't remotely interested

in Japan, nor had I ever wanted to be a sad western Buddhist. I'd always suspected that adopting an exotic religion might be a way of keeping uncomfortable truths at arm's length. But something about Sister Elaine's approach made me believe that Zen meditation could be a practical way forward. I even had a hunch that it might be a potent force against depression, though I couldn't have told you why at the time.

I needed something that was going to help me get through every day. I wasn't interested in theology or even in being good. I wanted a technique which could take me to the reality of things.

Tibetan Buddhists had been giving lectures in Cardiff and a lovely nun called Anila (they're all called that) had begun to teach us meditation using various visualisations. While I could see how this might be good for your heart rate, I couldn't take imagining Tibetan gods seriously. I mentioned this to Sister Elaine and said that I was suspicious of anything that relied so much on the imagination. As a writer, I knew how much wish-fulfilment might become involved. 'Fancy you knowing that', she commented.

Later I blurted out one of my greatest fears. If I learned to meditate properly, would that mean the end of my writing? Sister Elaine replied quite sharply, 'Why ever would it? The poetry comes from the best part of you, from the same place as the meditation.' I was so relieved that I began to cry. I hadn't known it was bothering me so much. A robin landed on the balcony outside and began to feed.

*

I tried to persuade Dr Parsons to let me go back to work after a few weeks but he insisted, rightly, that I was still far from well. 'Depression is a serious illness. Recovering from it is going to be like getting over a major operation.' But no matter how much people tried to make me think of it in physical terms – 'if you had a broken leg, you wouldn't feel bad about being off work, would you?' – I felt a deep shame about the fact I was going through it. We put 'post-viral debility' on the sick notes, hoping to keep the dreaded word 'depression' away from my personnel file.

I'll never forget the funeral of a family friend who killed himself in a depressed state. Suicide is often glossed over at memorial services, but our minister had the courage to be explicit in his address. He said, 'In middle age, there are dragons which have to be fought. And to be defeated in that battle is no shame.'

I believe this passionately about other people but I can't apply it to myself. In you, depression is a chemical misfortune. In me, it's the existential condition that I deserve because, at core, I'm a terrible person.

The local paper reported that a male African monkey had appeared in Roath, Cardiff, where there was a female on heat, kept in a cage. Nobody knew from where he'd escaped and nobody'd reported a monkey missing. Neighbours were feeding the male monkey bananas and nuts.

When people try to describe being depressed they often say that it's like losing colour from the world. This is true but approximate. Sometimes in old westerns, they would shoot night scenes in full sunlight but covering the camera lens with a blue filter. This gave an eerie 'moonlight' effect, in which you could see details in the whole landscape, including the lynch mob riding for the isolated farmstead. I understood the convention, but it never looked convincing to me. There was too much shadow in some places, too little in others.

This kind of shooting is called day-for-night. When you're depressed you live in eclipse light, that strange sepia when sparkle is dimmed and you can feel the pull of huge bodies of which you're normally unaware. It's the light of the past or, rather, the light of looking back at the past from the present.

It's daylight as it might be seen by a ghost.

*

My grandmother was a professional invalid. I was never quite sure why she'd taken to her bed, but I knew that depression was part of the mix.

She was a tyrannical patient. She was told to keep knitting so that her hands wouldn't seize up with rheumatoid arthritis. She refused and they did. My mother had a fright when the pills the doctor prescribed turned up in the commode, thinking they'd passed through her whole and that something was very wrong. It wasn't, she'd just decided not to take them. Mam-gu made my parents turn her bed so that her back was to the window. If she didn't like you she'd talk nothing but Welsh in front of you, even if you didn't understand it.

Once she sent my grandfather out to look for apricots. This was in west Wales in the 1950s and it was mid-winter.

In my bedroom in Cardiff, the dragons were still visiting. Every now and again the corrosive boredom of being awake intensified into what I can only call the Horrors.

It was like being pushed off a cliff. My mood would suddenly plunge and all my worst nightmares would flock round me, vicious and dangerous, as I had no defence against them. They were so strong they took my breath away. Leighton would watch me fall, not knowing what had happened. All I could hear was the wind roaring in my ears, the thin air dropping me and no sound would come out of my mouth's small 'o'.

> There can be no Good Will. Will is always Evil.
>
> William Blake, Annotations to Swedenborg's Wisdom of Angels
> Concerning Divine Love and Divine Wisdom, *Blake: Complete
> Writings*, ed Geoffrey Keynes (OUP, 1985), p. 89

When it came to willpower I was used to driving myself hard and took it for granted that I should be able to run two careers at the same time – one as a poet, the other working for the BBC. The financial independence this gave me from the literary world allowed me to write what I wanted, as opposed to what I thought might sell. I'd think nothing of getting up to do a day's writing before starting in the office at nine. And work there wasn't finished, as my boss said, 'until it's done'.

And yet now I couldn't even make myself walk to the shops. What the hell had happened?

Even the polite suggestion to myself that I should 'go out for a little walk' aroused such a sickening revolt in me that I knew that I could no longer rely on my willpower as an engine to drive my life. I'd have to find another mechanism that didn't involve an iron will. I'd have to convert from fossil fuels to renewable energy.

Two days before the Crash I'd visited friends on their farm in west Wales. The first question they always ask isn't 'How are you?' but 'Have you eaten?'. I love this, because it's the essence of civilisation – food first, culture later. After we'd eaten and caught up on the news – they always know more of the Cardiff gossip than I do – we went out to the big shed where the sheep are wintered. I was given a pair of wellies and we embarked on the usual fiction that I was helping them with farm work.

The shed was divided so that the sheep expecting triplets were in one pen, those carrying twins in another and so forth. Our job was to separate the ewes that weren't pregnant from the rest, which we did, using a system of railings and gates. Rhian explained that this had to be done so that they knew which sheep needed extra rations. The 'empty' ewes wouldn't be fed.

When I heard this I felt as though I'd been hit in the stomach. Rationally, I knew that what Rhian meant was that only the pregnant sheep would be given extra food, but that's not what I heard emotionally. In my stomach, what I understood was that childless women are useless and don't deserve to be nourished. I began to starve.

*

I'd become an energy black hole. I hadn't missed a single meal, did nothing more strenuous than get up from bed, walk downstairs to lie on the settee, and still I was losing weight by the pound. Something was drawing tremendous amounts of energy from my system.

Depression has been defined as 'fog over the battlefield'. I didn't have a clue what was going on inside me, except to know that some radical struggle was taking place and that it was best to keep my mind away from it.

I watched the light pacing round the room like a lion.

Whenever I had any energy at all I'd plot my escape. I'd decide to change everything in our life – we'd go abroad, I'd change career, dye my hair blonde, anything to be out of here before the Horrors came back.

'Go back to bed,' said Leighton sensibly. 'You can't even open a tin. We're fine as we are.'

*

Someone once told me 'Your worst nightmares always come true.' Being depressed has always been mine. That, and turning into my grandmother.

Mam-gu came to live with us when I was seven and her bed was in the living room downstairs. My sister and I rarely went in there. One day I ran downstairs and into the room, forgetting that Mam-gu was there and found the district nurse washing her. I was shocked by her wrinkly breasts and huge white torso, misshapen from years of being bed-ridden. She was a dead weight and lifting her in the middle of the night damaged my mother's back.

In that back parlour, Mam-gu became like a spider in her web of banging, rows and shouting. I don't have a single good memory of her.

Ever since then I've dreaded being such a dead weight, an oppressor of other people because of my own depression. At the height of an earlier episode I remember getting hysterical because I found a mark on my ankle like one Mam-gu had. I lay in the bath, sobbing. I was mortally afraid that I would turn into her, with a bottle of Lucozade by the bed and an invalid's rage at the healthy world. Now I was afraid that I was doing exactly the same to Leighton.

Most nights I'd wake up three or four times gasping for breath, feeling like I was suffocating. Cuts and scrapes refused to heal. My appetite vanished and my digestive system, which required abundant oxygen to metabolize food, failed to make use of much of what I forced myself to eat; instead my body began consuming itself for sustenance. My arms and legs gradually began to wither to sticklike proportions.

Jon Krakauer, *Into Thin Air*, (Anchor Books, 1997), p. 88

For some time past I've been reading a lot of mountaineering books. It's a fair bet that I'll never put foot to crampon because I suffer from vertigo, so I need other people to do my climbing for me. There's something about stories of endurance at high altitudes which reminds me of depression. The austerity of the sport leads to extreme perceptions. The view from the summit seldom seems to be the point for these climbers. They're driven up the mountain by compulsions beyond their control. The panorama they buy at such a high price is, nevertheless, of great value – like the expensive knowledge which comes through depression.

Even though he's discussing altitude sickness and not depression, I recognise something important in Jon Krakauer's description of his body consuming itself. As I tried to acclimatise to the new altitude at which I was living my life, I felt as though my body was cannibalising itself. I've never cared much for the idea of depression as anger turned inwards (denial, perhaps), but I must admit that I did feel as though, in the absence of any other object, I'd turned on myself.

Is depression, then, an emotional auto-immune disease? The body's defences treating its own emotions suddenly as alien and mounting an attack on them? Might self-aggression be an emotional style that could be mimicked by the body? My grandmother suffered from lupus and my depression seems to come from that side of the family. I wonder.

I think I've come up with a commercial idea. A depression tent. Modelled on the Native American menstruation tent, it's a one-person chamber in silk, including pillows and eiderdowns for the worst lows. Self-standing, the tent can be quickly and easily assembled in any room, providing shelter from intrusive relatives and acting as an emotional decompression chamber. Also available in: Black, Burgundy and Lilac. Care needs to be taken that the tent isn't used too often, or it might encourage escapism. For a premium, Luxury Bedouin versions are available. We could make a fortune.

*

AUTO-IMMUNITY (AUTO-ALLERGY)
Self-Tolerance

For many years it was assumed that the body would not make immunological response against components of its own tissues. In general, this assumption is correct ... Self-tolerance must be actively maintained, however, and it may break down, after which antibodies or the mechanisms of cell-mediated immunity may be directed against components of the body's own cells. This is commonly called auto-immunity although the term auto-allergy is more appropriate, since immunity in the ordinary sense of protection is not involved.

The New Encyclopaedia Britannica, 15th Edition,
Micropaedia, Vol IX, p. 257

I dreamt that a creature, a cross between a beaver and a rabbit had landed between my shoulder blades, biting in so deeply that it hung there. Whenever I moved to try and catch the creature its weight would make the flesh gape even more, as if it were unzipping my back.

'Get it off me!' I screamed at my mother, but she couldn't see a way of removing the beast without first pushing its teeth further in. I was frantic but every movement made things worse.

Of course, the creature on my back was me and it was pointless trying to get away. For as long as I can remember, I've felt allergic to myself. If you met me you'd think I was perfectly nice, but that's not what I'm talking about. It's what you are at two in the morning when you've been pushed off a cliff again and have nothing to hold on to as you fall.

Was I pushed, or did I jump? That's what this depression's about. For the moment, I reserved judgement and concentrated on surviving, still too concerned with the approaching landing to begin to look for clues.

There was something wrong with my internal communications system.

Instead of providing its usual steady narrative about what I was doing, what I should do, the commentary box in my head seemed to have a faulty connection. It had two modes: screaming and radio silence.

This news blackout was a very curious sensation. If my body was an empire there was a rebellion going on somewhere and natives had cut the telegraph wires. I could no longer impose my imperial will on whole areas of myself which used to obey me. I had no idea what was going on behind those enemy lines, and I suspected that later, when I was again able to map my territory, the shape of my possessions would have changed drastically.

*

There is no news today.

BBC news bulletin, Good Friday, 1930

(Quoted in John Davies, *Broadcasting and the BBC in
Wales*, (University of Wales Press, Cardiff, 1994), p. 192)

Whenever my mother gets depressed, she has a baking session. 'Out of the blues came forth sweetness' could be her
slogan. She's adventurous in confectionery and concocts
mango, pineapple and ginger mixtures for comfort. She's a
superb baker. As she passes over the tin-foiled contraband
she says every time 'It's not as good as usual', but that's
never true. Of course, I eat everything she brings us but,
unfortunately, it's not food you can live on.

And still I'd try to walk on my phantom limb, my collapsed
will power. I'd tell myself sternly that it was time to open
the curtains. I might as well have commanded myself to
abseil down a cliff:

'No way.'

'Go on!'

'Forget it.'

No matter how often I'd tell myself there was no physical reason why I couldn't get up, go for a stroll in the park, my body refused to believe it and mutinied.

I never used to think of my 'personality' as important until I lost it in depression. I thought it was a fairly superficial aspect of the character which expresses itself in the day-to-day quirkiness of your preferences for one kind of clothes over another. I love earrings, perfume, music and newspapers and refuse to buy a mobile phone or a microwave oven.

Depression wiped all this out of me. I didn't dress, ate anything that was put in front of me, watched *Blue Peter* and *Ricki Lake*, couldn't stand music. It was as if my personality files had been wiped. There was no way of knowing who I was any more, or who I might be when I finally got out of bed.

At the stage where I couldn't read or watch television, I sometimes felt like looking at pictures. I pulled out my post-cards (which I tend to collect) and leafed through art museum catalogues. But the most surprising and uncharacteristic development for me was a new-found liking for *Hello!* which I'd never bought before in my life. Perhaps because I was now being forced to live on the surface of my life, I found looking at the PR of celebrities oddly cheering. I liked the sheer human folly of people trying to persuade the world that they were happy. It was good to laugh at people for their pretensions, but I found it interesting because I'd been trying to prop myself up for so long that I knew what they were up to.

Leighton was so ashamed of buying the magazine at our local newsagent that he would hide it, like pornography, inside our *Western Mail*. 'Is your wife still ill?' the lady would ask every week. I think she'd stopped believing that he was buying it for me long before I was better.

> Why should you want to exclude any anxiety, any grief, any melancholy from your life, since you do not know what it is that these conditions are accomplishing in you.
>
> Rainer Maria Rilke, *Letters to a Young Poet*
> trs. Joan M. Burnham (New World Library, 1992), p. 85

The best part of *Hello!* isn't the glossy pages but what used to be the single black and white page in the middle of the magazine. This reports celebrity news stories in brief and they're always disasters – divorce, addiction, law suits, death. Here's the reality check which shows the rest of the magazine for what it really is: show business.

This depression's my own reality check. After years of faulty PR to myself, this is where the real story comes out.

CHAPTER TWO

Previous Convictions

It was twenty years before I realised that I believed I'd been cursed.

Looking back at it now, it's the only explanation that made sense: that an outside agent was sabotaging my inner life. No matter how far I ran from what I thought were the causes of my unhappiness – and I ran to America – it was as if my foot were tethered to a stake hammered into the ground of my past. If I strayed too far from it I'd feel a sharp tug and would find myself sprawled on the ground, floored by a desperation that I couldn't understand and didn't want.

The only possible explanation was that I was damned.

For me, poetry has always been about looking at life from a slightly off-centre point of view. One day when I was still a toddler, my mother had left me asleep in my cot and was doing her housework downstairs. The phone rang and it was the neighbour who lived behind us telling her that I was out on the window ledge of the back bedroom.

I had somehow managed to open the big window to our 1950s Wimpey house and was treading the slate ledge outside, looking in, arms and legs stretched out into an X against the glass.

When I was a teenager, we moved into a house, which looked over the whole of Cardiff, which is set into a crater leading down to the sea. At night I could hear everything, from the foghorns out in the Bristol Channel to the City Hall clock striking every quarter of an hour. I watched buses on their routes from town to the suburbs and at night I would lean out of the window of my bedroom, smelling the honeysuckle and wondering at the nebula of sodium lights below me, a glinting network of human relationships just beyond my grasp.

Sometimes, at dusk, when the windows of our house looked like blank eyes filled with the huge spaces of sunset, I'd lean out and look back in at my seventies bedroom, with its mismatched childhood furniture and *Lord of the Rings* posters.

I've never lost the sense of magic about leaning out of a window and looking back into the room you've left. It gives the objects inside, which are suffused with your smell, and are part of your dream life, a new objectivity. For a fraction of a second, you're able to see your own life without yourself in it.

This is what poetry has always been to me – a way of giving yourself a point of view outside your own seeing.

It's a toddler clinging to a windowsill, looking back at her horrified mother rushing towards her. And, later, it's about not falling.

I started to write poetry when I was seven years old. It came from nowhere and took root in my life almost without my being conscious of it.

One Easter holiday I was bored, stuck inside the house in wet weather and suddenly started to compose a long rhyming narrative poem. I still possess a copy of my first poem, which was an epic, describing the rain. It was execrable:

O mae'n bwrw glaw,	Oh it's raining
Mae dŵr ar fy llaw	There's water on my hand
Mae awr yn mynd	An hour has gone
O dyma fy ffrind.	Oh here's my friend.
. . . Dyma gawod arall eto	. . . Here's another shower
Rheda mewn i'r tŷ, Deio	Run into the house, Deio
O dyna dro gwael	Oh that's bad luck
Fi yw'r ail.	I came second.
. . . Glaw a baw, Glaw a baw	Rain and muck, Rain and muck
O Deio taw	Oh, Deio, shut up
Mae'r ieir yn y clos	The hens are in the yard
Mewn awr bydd yn nos.	In an hour it will be dark.

My rain poem was written on the back of the Cardiff Port Sanitary Authority Public Health (Imported Food) Regulations, 1925, where my father worked as an environmental health officer. On each sheet I had also undertaken 'not to use or sell' a specified food 'for human consumption in compliance with the above regulations.'

Some of what I learned that Easter was what didn't work in prosody. I came to grief on the name 'Mic' (Mick) as an end-rhyme and I had crossed out this failed stanza with a big frustrated red asterisk. It looks like a fatal spider hanging poisonously in the middle of the manuscript.

I can't remember what possessed me to start such a venture. Day after day I'd work on the dining-room table. This poem made me happier than anything I knew. The project of getting the real world into a pattern that sounded beautiful thrilled me deeply and made up, in a way, for the washout of a holiday. Unable to go out on the sopping lawn, I'd found another form of play which fascinated me more and that could be practised, whatever the weather.

The most exciting events in the poem are that it stops raining and that Deio is caught smoking. The plot is hardly scintillating but what's good about the work is its remorseless drive to rhyme. In fact, the rhyme seems to drive the plot completely, introducing the Old Lady of Cidweli (to rhyme with 'gwely', bed) and even Calfari (Calvary, to not quite rhyme with 'taranu', to thunder).

What interests me now, looking at the manuscript, are the corrections which my mother made to my magnum opus. A teacher, she's physically incapable of reading anything without a pen in her hand. She used a red biro and printed amendments over my draft, with its seven-year-old handwriting. She regularised the spelling (a service I still need today) and put in punctuation.

But she went even further. For me, this adventure in rhyme was immensely exciting and I wasn't looking for strict regularity. Mam standardised some of the lines, so that they were regular syllabically, a habit that I would tend to undo in my work today. Even further, she sometimes changed the plot, replacing my infant chattiness with more poetic words like 'orchard'. This well-meaning rewriting had undone the most promising aspect of the poem – the way I was willing to subordinate reality to the required rhyme scheme. You can always learn to rhyme well later but, unless you have that compulsive pleasure in consonant sound, to the point of nonsense, you'll never be a poet.

This was the start of a blurring of the borders between me and my mother. Poetry, for me, has always been my sacred place, where I allow myself to express my true feelings, however absurd, exaggerated, or 'uncool'. Of course, the text can be improved later, but the first flush of enthusiasm has to be totally uncensored, of no use to anybody or anything – including yourself – the only rationale for its existence being the sheer joy of it. Even today the best reason I can give for writing poetry is that there's nothing in it for me.

My mother is from west Wales, where the eisteddfod tradition of artistic competitions was very strong. She encouraged me to enter all kinds of poetic competitions in order to develop my talent. This certainly helped me to learn creative discipline and the skill of writing to a deadline and on a set topic. But she was always much more keen on the competition aspect of things than I was, which made me most uneasy. The upside, however, was that if I won, I was well in with her for some time, which was a blessing.

My mother could be moody and unpredictable. Sometimes, enraged, usually by something I'd done, she'd disappear into her bedroom for a few days. I didn't understand why I had such an effect on her and caused us all so much misery. My misbehaviour caused our whole domestic world to fall apart and, because I seemed to cause these crises so often, I felt like a pariah within the family. I concluded that I must be wicked.

I understood later that this was Mam suffering from depression herself: the inability to cope, the wretchedness, the despair. I once saw a fascinating article by Margaret Drabble about depression saying that a child needs a mother against whom she can kick in order to develop a healthy sense of self-confidence. This becomes impossible if the mother is unwell or depressed – you'd have to be inhuman to put the boot in when someone you love is in such obvious but inexplicable pain. So I'd shut up, swallow my sense of injustice and wait for the natural mood upswing which always came in a couple of days.

If I wrote a tentative draft of a poem – which I often did after the lights were turned out at night – Mam would sometimes revise it with me. My 'splurge' would be messy, disordered, but would contain the essential electricity for a poem. Looking back it now seems a rare luxury for a writer to have such a close reader. However, this mother-and-daughter composition wasn't a relationship between equals and, while I was pleased to see my work improving and to learn editing skills, I came to feel like a fraud. Somehow Mam's 'improving' my most intimate sentiments was a violation of an important border between us.

My reaction to this whole set-up became clouded with shame. Shame for depending so much on my mother and, also, shame for the work that I did without her. I remember writing one short essay in school when I was ten about the robbers crucified with Christ. An instinctively religious child, I was convinced that the three TV masts I could see on the Wenallt hill just outside Cardiff were the three crosses in Jerusalem. The disparity in place and time puzzled me a little, but I had to believe the evidence of my own eyes. The crosses were there.

As I was writing I found myself swept up imaginatively in the subject and carried along on an almost sexual sensation, as I saw the scene vividly in front of me. I was given nine out of ten for the essay and, to my distress, it was read out to the rest of the class. Had I known that was to happen I'd have censored myself ruthlessly. In shame, I tore out the essay from my notebook and threw it away, though I've often wished I could see it again and judge it with older eyes. I bet it was good.

*

It was that year, when I was ten, that the inevitable teasing began in school. I must have been an easy target – sensitive, a swot, and far too good at homework to be in any way part of the gang. I took the taunts to heart, even though they were no more than children's routine cruelties. I still can't say it was character-forming, but I eventually understood the importance of these people when the great Russian poet, Joseph Brodsky told us, in his poetry class at Columbia University, to beware of 'the mockers'. These, he said, were the critical voices that made fun of the poet's rapture and, when internalised, became a powerful force for self-censorship. Giving in to them would mean allowing ten-year-olds, with their brutal conformism, to win over an adult's creative projects. Also, for a poet, being afraid of being tasteless or over-the-top may avoid minor embarrassments but will certainly hold major insights at arm's length. Looking for guaranteed safety is the most dangerous project of all.

These bullies, though, led me unintentionally to make a huge discovery about writing and how it can turn the tables on people. I was so unhappy on the island of eight desks where I had to sit that I began to outline a play in my notebook as a form of escapism. Looking around the class, I made a list of the characters my classmates might play in the performance that I envisaged. I included everyone, even my enemies, because now I was looking at my situation from an artistic point of view, and my judgement was entirely different. This is why writing anything is a form of forgiveness. My judgement now wasn't based on whether I liked people or if they were nice to me or not, but on the qualities they could bring to my play.

Children have no privacy and my classmates soon began to ask me what I was doing. I wouldn't tell them, and the more occupied I became with the first act of the drama, the more interested were my tormentors. They craned over my shoulder to see the dramatis personae. Eventually, I told them the idea. Everybody wanted to know what his or her part was and whether or not it was a good one.

What I was doing was the creative version of leaning out of my bedroom window in order to gain a different view of the painful situation inside. But I had unexpectedly discovered vulnerability in my persecutors – their vanity. They wanted to be part of something original, even though they mocked the person who produced it. They became very uneasy when they feared that they would be excluded.

This was the first time I'd come across the very ambivalent feelings some people have towards writers – a combination of jealousy towards their ability to invent a world away from everybody else and a desire to thump it out of them.

Anybody who was with me in school knows that this pattern continued for many years. I'd enter competitions, win them and draw unwanted teasing. Interestingly, this was never from the less academically able, with whom I got on well (I was considered a 'nice swot') but from those who were snapping at my heels in the competitions. One year, one of my classmates wrote a bitchy piece in the school magazine and I snapped. I came home, told my mother that I wasn't going to compete any more, that I was taking myself out of the arena.

This pulled a hornet's nest down on my head and provoked the worst row I'd ever had at home. My mother pushed, cajoled, bullied and reproached but all to no purpose. It was more important to me to be left alone than to win. Mam's usual blackmail didn't work and I recall her saying bitterly, 'Our relationship will never be the same again.' It wasn't.

Mam was right about the writing, but for the wrong reason. I began a silence in poetry of nearly seven years and walked into a danger of which I had no idea and which damaged me nearly beyond repair.

They say that language develops in infants as the baby finds itself alone and calls for its absent mother. At its very root, then, language is about needing your mother and about responding to your desolation without her. It's surprising how many poets lost their mothers early, suggesting that 'mother tongue' is far more than a figure of speech. Poetry allows you to speak to those people you can't in real life because they're dead or out of reach in another way.

The lesson I had learned so far about poetry was that it led people to make demands that I didn't want to meet and that they hated you for being good at it. I hadn't yet worked out the combination of contempt and admiration in every bully's view of his or her victim. I didn't have the sense to take other people's discomfiture in this as a sign that I might be doing something very right, rather than the opposite.

In *Black Sun*, Julia Kristeva makes a fascinating connection between language acquisition and depression. Her argument is tightly packaged in the cult terminology of psychoanalytic deconstruction, but the basic story, as far as I can decode it, goes like this: In her early life a child believes that she's God and that her every need is supplied by the world on her own terms. She's hungry, a breast appears; lonely, and a face looms over the cot. Suddenly, one day, the child finds herself alone. She begins to feel bereft but, instead of mourning her mother, she calls for her. The new tactic works and the mother appears in response to language. So, the child learns words to enable her to manipulate the world but, in the process, skips an essential stage of grieving for her independent mother. Language is acquired at the cost of grief. The infant has lost her mother but found her again in language, thus masking the original loss.

Through her language skills, the daughter isn't aware that she has lost the mother because she can speak to and about her. Any unconscious rage at the breast that disappeared is directed not at the true mother but at her symbolic representative in language, which is now part of the child. This may be why depressed people hate themselves so much. It's too dangerous to turn that rage on the mother – that would make the depressed person face a grief they fear would overwhelm them – so it's easier to hate the mother who's been symbolically absorbed into the patient's self through language.

For a poet, this theory has another fascinating implication. If language is a child's way of evading coming to terms with depression, how much more true must this be of a poet who has schooled herself in fluency and technique for years? Verbal virtuosity might serve to further postpone the real emotional crisis underneath. Might not being bilingual in this instance become a way of evading the experience of despair to an even greater degree, as the poet would have so much more linguistic delight to distract her before crashing against depression's blank wall?

In depression I find myself beyond words, beyond sense, beyond beauty even. And yet, the two – depression and poetry – are deeply interconnected. Depression has pushed me out of the window of my own life. It will help me, if only I can climb safely back in, to start living according to a new and more real point of view.

A truly bilingual person has not one mother tongue, but two. Welsh was my blood mother, English my stepmother.

People look at me, astonished, when I tell them that I grew up in Cardiff in the 1960s and 1970s and hardly ever spoke

English. We spoke Welsh at home and in school. Ballet was English, as were friends on the estate where we lived, but social life, chapel and youth club were all Welsh-speaking.

When I went up to Cambridge for my admission interview, my father and I spoke English all the way in the car because I needed the practice. My written English had won me a first in Practical Criticism on the entrance exam, I learnt later, but I was unsure of my verbal fluency. After I went up I was very aware that my spoken English wasn't as muscular as that of my friends, so I started a vocabulary book, to try and catch up. It included words that I didn't know: desultory, anodyne, recalcitrant, vagaries – all the puff words so loved by eighteen- and nineteen-year-olds studying English.

You can't inhabit a language until you've loved in it. I only started speaking English well when I met and fell in love with R. I date my drama with my stepmother tongue from then and it was just as bloody as the struggle with my mother had been. R and I were instantly inseparable and walked around like a creature with four legs, attached at the hip. It was the high drama of first love and we saw ourselves as the inhabitants of Yeats's poem:

> The woods were round them, and the yellow leaves
> Fell like faint meteors in the gloom . . .

We knew that

> Before us lies eternity; our souls
> Are love, and a continual farewell.

WB Yeats, 'Ephemera', WB Yeats: The Poems,
ed Richard J. Finneran (Macmillan, New York, 1983), p. 15

You get the picture.

If I had the traditional female difficulty in drawing a line between my mother's wants and myself, all immigration controls were suspended when I met R. He walked into my life past deserted border posts. By the end, I couldn't tell the difference between his face and mine.

Having given up writing, my hold on my own beliefs had already been loosened. R was a strong character and I was more than willing to follow in his slipstream. One of my tutors met him and remarked: 'That young man is a tiger!' Once I'd given myself away, I saw little point in hanging on to anything – neither pride, dignity nor independence.

One weekend R went home, leaving me in college. Without him I just stopped living. I sat in his room, in the middle of his books and shoes, unable to read or think of anything but when he'd be back. I found it hard to breathe without him.

The stakes were high, making this relationship exciting, volatile, and larger-than-life. This didn't mean it was always happy, but it was mythologically compelling. I was asking R to carry my life for me, an expectation which was bound to end in disappointment and grief. I didn't feel real without him. I remember one time being in the graveyard of an old church in Glamorgan, in a mad mood at dusk. We were wretched about something and in the middle of one of our scenes I lay down on a double tombstone, as if it were a bed, said, 'Come on, you too'. He refused, commenting that somebody had to keep their feet on the ground.

Cracks appeared in the relationship fairly early on. After about five months of unquestioning bliss, and of doing no academic work whatsoever, second-year exams were looming and I wanted to do some studying. R poured scorn on anybody who worked consistently as a 'plodder', someone who had opted out of the challenge of living. But for me, reading and understanding, say, the work of George Eliot or Milton was a crucial part of who I wanted to be. In order to write you have, first, to be a reader. R was sociable, always at the centre of a group; I needed to spend time alone. Our conflicts hardened into fixed positions – he said I was ambitious, calculating, puritanical, afraid of real life and under my parents' thumb. I soon became bored with the drifting life of pubs and chat, but I couldn't do without his approval.

My mother and R hated each other on sight. He lit up a cigarette in the house without asking permission and she ended up refusing to speak English whenever he was there. They fought over me like cats. I tried to make them both part of my life but they were oil and water and refused to be mixed. In the end the power struggle became so intense that I felt myself disappear between them.

I wasn't sorry that my being with R riled my mother so much: it was one clear way I could distinguish between her and myself. But the situation soon became unsustainable. If I seemed to be following my mother's values, R became resentful and intolerant. At home I wasn't able to share any of my college life, even when I had problems, because R was such a central part of it. I had two languages – Welsh and English – at each other's throats and I was in the middle, under unbearable pressure. To admit that the relationship with R was anything less than perfect would have proved my mother right. I was too stubborn to give her that satisfaction. To criticise my mother offended my natural loyalty towards my family and made me feel very uneasy, as I was more eager to please my parents than to be well myself.

That's when I saw the angry spider of my first poem again. I'd come down with glandular fever at the end of my first year at Cambridge and was delirious. I hallucinated that a big black spider was sitting in the middle of my face so that I was looking at the world through horror. At that time seeing a real spider made me hysterical. Spiders looked like unpredictable hands that wanted too much intimacy. The big black shape over my face made my vision crazed like a shattered windscreen. If only I'd known it, this was a huge Dead End sign, a warning that this world of conflict between home and love had, somehow, to come to an end or it would finish me off.

I chose to ignore it and had to suffer far more before learning this spider lesson. Nowadays, a silver spider in a web is my good-luck charm – a calamity turned into good fortune. Like depression.

I desperately wanted to start writing poetry again, but failed. Cambridge, with its emphasis on honing the critical skills, was hardly the place to give you confidence in your own work. I did try writing in English once, but the content of the poem made R so angry that I completely lost my nerve. I had been spending time with a friend of mine who fancied me and had written about the drama of a moment of romantic potential that had come to nothing. R found and read my poem and was, understandably, livid. By the end of our row, however, I'd eaten so much humble pie that I was scared off poetry for years. I couldn't help feeling that I'd been hung for a lamb that I hadn't even stolen.

R once dreamt that I was very excited about an idea I'd had for a novel. Then I took my clothes off and that was the novel. The message I internalised was that it was all right to be creative, as long as that energy went into your relationship. Otherwise, it was dangerous.

Poetry had started as a pastime on a wet afternoon, a game to play. I didn't realise then, as I slotted in rhymes to names, writing on the red chenille tablecloth, that I was playing with a dangerous substance, one that would take its revenge on me if I didn't honour it with work. What's at stake with poetry for me is awareness of my own life. Without writing, I'm unable to exercise a kind of inner eye, a moral vision which allows me to make sense of how I'm living. Everybody carries around in their heads a store of images, rules, scraps of experience which help them to make choices at important junctures in their lives. This is the raw material of poetry and everybody treasures it, even if they have no intention of turning it into art.

This source is like an inner spring, which takes a great deal of time to trickle into a pool at which you can drink. It needs privacy to build up, a protective wall around it. To be without this inner nourishment is to be a barren person, able only to react to life as you drift through it, with no inner direction. Draw too much on it and you exhaust yourself. If you don't use it, the water becomes stagnant and you can't see anything through it.

Wisdom's ecosystem hasn't changed over the ages, although our names for it have. This is why the twelfth-century mystic, Bernard of Clairvaux's advice to his followers still holds today:

> But here we must take heed of two dangers; that of giving to others what is meant for ourselves and of keeping to ourselves what is given us for others. You are certainly retaining for yourself that which belongs to your neighbour, for instance, if you are given the gifts of knowledge or of eloquence – but fear, perhaps, or self-consciousness, or sloth, or an ill-judged humility restrains your good gift of speech in a useless, or rather, blameable silence. On the other hand, you dissipate and lose that which is your own if, before you have received a complete inpouring from God, while you are, so to speak, but half-filled, you rush to pour yourself forth . . . Indeed what you thus communicate is merely the vomit which is swelling within yourself . . . If you are wise

you will show yourself as a reservoir rather than as a canal. For a canal spreads abroad water as it receives it, but a reservoir waits until it is full before overflowing and so gives, without loss to itself, its superabundant water.

(Quoted in Anne Bancroft, *The Luminous Vision: Six Medieval Mystics and their Teachings*, (Mandala, London, 1989), pp. 95–6

With R I had certainly given what, perhaps, was meant for myself, without knowing it. But because I loved him, I didn't think I needed anything else. If you'd asked R, he'd have said that he liked and respected poetry. He wrote a thesis on the heartbreaking work of rural poet John Clare one year, but he had no understanding at all of the life that's required in order to make poems. He was religious-minded but without faith, liked poetry but hated the discipline it demanded. The poet needs to be totally open to suggestions from the unconscious, however shocking, whereas R, like my mother, had strong views on what was sound and what was not. Getting ready to write is like carrying water round in a saucer over bumpy ground, trying not to spill a drop. This means holding something back from other people, even your loved ones. It means listening closely to your inner voices and trusting them, giving attention for long periods of time to ideas that might never work out, nurturing a privacy that sometimes takes precedence over being a couple. Poets are not easy partners.

A short poem called 'In Dispraise of Poetry' by Jack Gilbert, which I found in an Australian writing centre's guest book, catches this ruinous side of poetry perfectly:

When the King of Siam disliked a courtier
he gave him a beautiful white elephant.
The miracle beast deserved such ritual
that to care for him properly meant ruin.
Yet to care for him improperly was worse.
It appears the gift could not be refused.

Poetry is my lie-detector test, the best way I have of detecting my own bullshit. It's better than therapy, than conversations with friends and is comparable in accuracy only to prayer. If I'm unsure what I think of a situation and try to write a poem about it, I'm able to make sense of it. Any lies in my thinking, any self-indulgence simply won't scan and I have to abandon them and move on to what will work practically, both in the poem and in my life. Poetry represents the minimum amount of reality that I require to live well. Without it, what I'm living isn't my genuine life but a forgery. It may look plausible but it wasn't meant for me.

Poetry has acquired a fluffy image, which is totally at odds with its real nature. It's not pastel colours, but blood-red and black. If you don't obey it as a force in your life, it will tear you to pieces.

This is because it's a form of energy, which links the electricity of your truth to the world around you. Metre and rhyme help to earth that energy and to find a safe way of embodying it in words. The raw materials of poetry link the trivia in your life to your deepest subconscious, so abusing the process is likely to cause you big psychological problems. If you don't do what your poetry wants you to, it will be out to get you. Unwritten poems are a force to be feared.

Although I'd given up poetry consciously, it hadn't left my dream life. In a notebook I wrote:

> Have been racked by dreams of guilt and violence. Last night poetry was out to get me. I had to foresee the blows and avoid them.
>
> 1. Through a pane of glass, to which I had my back, coming through with a pick-axe which melted the pane and my skull like ice, like a drip from a hot water tap.
> 2. Standing at a bus stop, it comes at me with a curved axe, with a sweeping movement from behind, using the haft's weight to make the blow accurate.

I ran from this frightening force, which seemed to demand more honesty than I was willing to give. Experience had presented me with a choice between being acceptable to others and being a poet and I'd chosen the former.

The Furies are the creative processes' revenge if you refuse to embody them in your life. This refusal is more than creative sabotage, it's impiety. The gods always avenge these. Greek mythology understood this psychological mechanism very precisely. Oedipus commits sacrilege by killing his father and sleeping with his mother. He's accountable for this, even though he didn't know what he was doing at the time. Ignorance of the spiritual laws is no excuse when a violation of this magnitude is committed. Oedipus is pursued relentlessly by the Furies, three crones who give him no peace and nearly drive him mad. I imagine them as a psychic force, an interference of voices, cacophonous music, psychedelic delusions, an emotional tinnitus. Their job is to avenge matricide. Killing the source of poetry in you is an offence against the gods because it shows contempt for the strongest force of truth in your life. It's like killing the best part of yourself. It's an act that requires penance and the perpetrator isn't easily absolved.

Having switched off poetry and refused to open myself to it again, I thought that life would be straightforward. But it wasn't. I used to have fantasies of becoming invisible and disappearing into a womb-like cubby-hole in the wall. I became morbidly self-conscious, fearing that people were laughing at me. I'd bought a pair of burgundy cowboy ankle boots which were, admittedly, 'striking' but which gave me great joy. One night, walking home from the bus stop in front of two fellow students, I became convinced that they were making fun of my somewhat individual boots. I never wore them again.

Instead of making my identity more strongly defined, the conflict between R and my mother had made me into a complete cipher. I no longer knew who I was or what I thought. I had no personal style and no weapons with which I could defend myself.

It came to a head in our college bar one night. I'd been persuaded to come down for a drink, after feeling rotten for a few days – unable to work or to enjoy myself. Suddenly I froze. It was as if the background noise of chat in the room suddenly became stone-heavy, too real, and it petrified me physically and emotionally.

The college pastoral machinery kicked into action and, when I could move, I was taken to my room, given my only mogadon ever and put to bed. I asked for R and my tutor very kindly drove down to town in her Mini to get him. He came straight away. I was distraught and insisted on sleeping in his pyjamas so, because it was February and freezing cold, he had no choice but to pull on my schoolgirlish nightie. When the duty nurse of the all-female college came to see me in the morning, she directed her questions at the invalid chain-smoking in her nightie until I, fully dressed, said in a wounded voice, 'It's not *him* who's gone mad, it's me.'

I decided to take some time out of college to sort myself out. After I'd regained my strength I moved out of my parents' house and into strange lodgings with an artist and his family in the Cathays area of Cardiff. There was a dead bird cremated onto a baking tray under my bed and a fox's head decomposing in a bucket tied to the top of the washing line.

R and I didn't survive that period, as I found my feet again. During the rest of my time at Cambridge we repeatedly tried getting together again but it was a disaster. All that was left was a mutual struggle, a battle of wills, which became totally draining. I hurt him as much as he hurt me. It became difficult to tell fear, pain and love apart.

*

After my degree I knew that my top priority had to be to start writing again. I couldn't do this while I felt torn by personal and cultural pressures. I needed neutral ground and so decided to go to America. I applied for scholarships and was awarded a Harkness Fellowship to study at Harvard.

The summer before I left for Harvard, R and I had got back together yet again. One day, I was listening to a David Bowie album and leaning out of the window of his room. It suddenly hit me with the impact of a truck that I wasn't making him happy and never could. This was the first time I'd been unselfish enough to think of the relationship from his point of view. I packed my bags and, again for the first time, left of my own accord.

The end of August arrived, with its departure date for the States and R came to see me off at Paddington. I loved hats at that time and was pushing a heap of suitcases on a trolley, with three hats piled on top of each other.

'The thing about you', he said casually, 'is that you've already given your heart away.'

At the time I took very little notice of these words, distracted as I was by final hugs and the awkwardness of heavy baggage. The statement made no sense. I wouldn't be surprised if R doesn't even remember saying it. Was he saying that he had my heart? Then why wasn't he looking after it? If it wasn't in my own breast, where was it? Was this simply a roundabout way of calling me a heartless bitch? There was no logical reason in the world why, now that we were finished, I should give a damn what he thought of me, except for my old habit of relying on him for my opinion of myself.

But below the level of reason, even of consciousness, the words lodged in me like a metal splinter. I despaired of ever being a viable person. I believed R's nonsense, which made me even more culpable than he was.

The hardest curse to lift is one you've placed on yourself.

CHAPTER THREE

Basic Investigative Guidelines

1 Don't attempt the Bible, *War and Peace*, or *À la Recherche du Temps Perdu*

On no account read Robert Burton's *Anatomy of Melancholy* when you're actually depressed. If ever a work of art was designed to defeat someone going through an episode of clinical depression, this tome is it. The book is long, written in interminable paragraphs and is designed to make you feel ignorant. It's basically a man showing off his knowledge of madness, a subject about which you already know too much. It will do you far more good to buy a copy of *Hello!* I've no doubt that Burton's collection of stories and opinions was considered highly amusing in the seventeenth century, but they had a different idea of entertainment then. I did, however, like the description of a possessed woman in volume one:

> Katherine Gualter, a cooper's daughter, *anno* 1571 . . . had such strange passions and convulsions, three men could not sometimes hold her; she purged a live eel . . . a foot and a half long . . . but the eel

---

afterwards vanished; she vomited some twenty-four pounds of fulsome stuff of all colours, twice a day for fourteen days; and after that she voided great balls of hair, pieces of wood, pigeon's dung, parchment, goose dung, coals; and after them two pounds of pure blood, and then again coals and stones, of which some had inscriptions, bigger than a walnut, some of them pieces of glass, brass, etc., besides paroxysms of laughing, weeping and ecstasies ... They could do no good on her by physic, but left her to the clergy.

Robert Burton, *The Anatomy of Melancholy*, ed Holbrook Jackson (Vintage, New York, 1977), First Partition, p. 201

The *Anatomy* is a compendium of learning on melancholy from classical times to the seventeenth century. As a practical handbook on depression it is somewhat lacking. Take this pearl of wisdom:

In the belly of a swallow, there is a stone found called chelidonius, 'which if it be lapped in a fair cloth, and tied to the right arm, will cure lunatics, madmen, make them amiable and merry.'

ibid, Second Partition, p. 218

Great. Now all I have to do now is catch a swallow. Another gem is this recipe for a face pack:

It is good overnight to anoint the face with hare's blood, and in the morning to wash it with strawberry and cowslip water, the juice of distilled lemons, juice of cucumbers, or to use the seeds of melons, or kernels of peaches beaten small, or the roots of arum, and mixed with wheat-bran to bake it in an oven,

and to crumble it in strawberry-water, or to put
fresh cheese-curds to a red face.   *ibid*, p. 254

I can see the therapeutic value of cosmetic pampering but I
don't think Leighton would go for hare's blood left on all
night. Burton goes on:

Piso commends a ram's lungs applied hot to the
fore-part of the head, or a young lamb divided in
the back, extenterated, etc.; all acknowledge the chief
cure to consist in moistening throughout.

ibid, p. 249

I'll stick to Nivea.

A note on the word 'melancholy'

Before it became picturesque, this word was a technical term
for the condition of having too much black bile in your
system of humours (black bile being one of the four chief
fluids or 'cardinal humours' of the ancient and medieval
physiologists). It also meant plain bad temper or sadness and
depression of spirits.

In the early Elizabethan period an affectation of melancholy was 'a favourite pose among those who made claim to
superior refinement' (*Oxford English Dictionary*). This is
when it became a word for tossers, an aestheticised version
of what the poet Robert Lowell called 'the Flats'. It's a tarted-
up version of sheer misery. Anyone who uses the word

melancholy for depression in the twenty-first century is secretly relishing the condition because at least it shows they're sensitive.

The Anatomy of Melancholy is a book for people who want to read about depression rather than those who suffer from it. However, it does contain a number of important clues which might be of use to the detective-depressive committed to tracking down the perpetrator of his or her own murder.

Burton is quite correct in specifying that depression is a disease of the imagination. This means that the depressive suffers from a faulty mechanism in the way he or she pictures reality, is a forger of his or her own life. Cognitive therapists focus on getting patients to see the glass as half-full rather than half-empty. Being positive has become rather a fetish. A more radical tactic would be to abolish the need for evaluation at all and just accept the glass as it is, whether it be cracked or brimming.

The absurdity of exercises in positivity is shown by the injunctions I found in a little book, *The Influence of Habits*, written by Canon Raymond de Saint Laurent and published by Aubanel in Dublin, 'Printers to His Holiness the Pope', Number 17 in their *Mind Training Series in* 1955. Canon de Saint Laurent condemns pessimism as a bad habit and urges the glum one to change his way of life:

> He should direct his thoughts towards new horizons. Where heretofore he was seeing everything black, he must now force himself to see it rose-coloured . . .

> The pessimist will soon get used to this new mental slant and he should apply himself to creating around him an atmosphere of optimism.
>
> No longer should he frequent 'the world of bores', but rather that in which healthy gaiety reigns.
>
> He should read books that deal with joy, dash and courage . . .
>
> He should even force himself to sing gay and lively refrains, especially at moments when depression threatens to engulf him.   *op cit*, pp. 83–84

Any attempt to cheer yourself up with positive thinking if you're genuinely depressed will only prolong the agony. And as for singing a cheerful tune, you can shove that.

Burton notes, accurately that 'Melancholy, the subject of our present discourse, is either in disposition or habit' (The First Partition, p. 143). To this statement I would add 'or both'. As far as I can see, there are three elements at play in any serious depressive episode. It seems certain that a tendency to depression can be genetically inherited, which is no surprise to sufferers who can trace the dark thread through their own families. Secondly, a localised lack of serotonin in the brain chemistry – induced by stress, drug use or a number of other causes – leads to the actual sensation of sickness in the patient. Thirdly, even the smallest emotional habits contribute hugely to whether we are optimists or pessimists from day to day. Practised habitually, these unconscious gestures harden into an attitude and, if they're false in any way or oppressive to us, can have a precipitating effect on any chemical discomfort sloshing around in the brain. These habits, in themselves, are only the slither of a few grains of sand down a slope but, taken all together, and in volatile chemical and emotional conditions, they become the mudslide of full depression.

It would be surprising if Burton never contradicted himself in a book the length of *The Anatomy of Melancholy* and in discussion of such a paradoxical disease. He concludes, with good reason, that depression is caused both by under- and over-activity. To my mind these aren't contradictions so much as descriptions of two different stages.

Burton notes that underactivity is a habit which can precipitate an auto-immune emotional reaction in an individual:

> As fern grows in untilled grounds, and all manner
> of weeds, so do gross humours in an idle body . . .
> A horse in a stable that never travels, a hawk in a
> mew that seldom flies, are both subject to diseases;
> which, left unto themselves, are most free from any
> such encumbrances. An idle dog will be mangy, and
> how shall an idle person think to escape? Idleness
> of the mind is much worse than this of the body;
> wit without employment is a disease . . . the rust of
> the soul, a plague, a hell itself . . . In a common-
> wealth, where is no public enemy, there is, likely,
> civil wars, and they rage upon themselves: this body
> of ours, when it is idle and knows not how to bestow
> itself, macerates and vexeth itself with cares, griefs,
> false fears, discontents, and suspicions: it tortures
> and preys upon his own bowels, and is never at rest.
>
> *op cit*, The First Partition, pp. 243–44

What is this but a description of depression as an auto-immune disease?

In a section entitled 'Superfluous Industry' Burton describes the will turned outward on the world, doing everything it can to avoid feeling melancholy – this is the frantic activity before the Crash:

> Another must have roses in winter, *alieni temporis flores* [flowers out of season] snow-water in summer, fruits before they can be or are usually ripe, artificial gardens and fish-ponds on the tops of houses, all things opposite to the vulgar sort, intricate and rare, or else they are nothing worth. So busy, nice, curious wits make that insupportable in all vocations, trades, actions, employments, which to duller apprehensions is not offensive, earnestly seeking that which others as scornfully neglect. Thus through our foolish curiosity do we macerate ourselves, tire our souls, and run headlong, through our indiscretion, perverse will, and want of government, into many needless cares and troubles, vain expenses, tedious journeys, painful hours; and when all is done, *quorsum haec? cui bono*? to what end?   *ibid*, pp. 367–68

This reminds me of my grandmother sending my grandfather out for apricots in winter. But this is also an excellent description of the norm of modern life, say, in New York, with instant gratification being used addictively as a way not to feel misery. Depressive habits of mind are acted out not only in individuals but also in whole societies.

Generally, with Burton, the fewer quotations in the text,

the more original his thinking. The most useful part of the *Anatomy* comes in the Third Partition, the subsection on 'Religious Melancholy'. As you would expect, Burton takes the standard Christian line, declaring that the 'last and greatest cause of this malady is our own conscience, sense of our sins, and God's anger justly deserved, a guilty conscience for some foul offence formerly committed'. (*op cit*, p. 400)

If this were true, why aren't all the bastards under the sun permanently depressed? I'm too much of a child of the psychiatric age to know that it isn't the fact of sin but our perception of it (a very different matter) that's relevant in this case. In the long section on the 'Cure of Melancholy', Burton is again off the depressive mark as he outlines proverbs designed to help a man lead a generally good life, as if virtue were a guarantee against depression. For example, he urges us to

> Be content with thy lot. Trust not wealth, beauty, nor parasites, they will bring thee to destruction. Have peace with all men, war with vice. Be not idle. Look before you leap . . . Admire not thyself. Be not proud or popular. Insult not . . . Fear not that which cannot be avoided. Grieve not for that which cannot be recalled. Undervalue not thyself . . . Take heed of a reconciled enemy. If thou come as a guest, stay not too long . . . Marry not an old crone or a fool for money. Be not over solicitous or curious. Seek that which may be found. Seem not greater than thou art. Take thy pleasure soberly. *Ocymums ne terito* [do not grind clover].

> *op cit*, Second Partition, pp. 204–5

Ah. Grinding clover. I knew I shouldn't have done it.

For Burton, the crux of the whole matter is not God's wrath, but the melancholic's lack of faith, which makes him misdoubt 'God's mercies'. This lets him fall into the hands of the Furies, Burton's name for an over-scrupulous conscience. 'Night and day', Burton translates from Juvenal, 'they carry the accusing witness in their own breast' (Third Partition, p. 401). This is a perfect description of the out-of-date ghosts which haunt the depressive and drive him or her mad. The depressive's problem isn't knowing the difference between moral right and wrong, so much as learning to recognise the difference between what's true and what's false in their own emotional lives. This is the real task for the depression detective.

I noticed in the paper that the Society of Chief Librarians is piloting 'a new way of classifying library books, listing them on content, style and setting ... aimed at enabling borrowers to indulge their literary appetites according to their mood.' (*Daily Telegraph*, 9 March, 1999). I like the idea of an anti-depressant corner in a library, as long as the books were chosen by someone who knows that 'upbeat' doesn't necessarily equal 'cheering'.

The books on my private 'take-heart' shelf are all books about transformation: Stella Gibbons's *Cold Comfort Farm*, Anita Loos's *Gentlemen Prefer Blondes* and E. Annie Proulx's *The Shipping News*. Everybody will have their own favourites.

2 Don't join a gym for the first time in fifteen years

The beneficial effects of exercise-induced endorphins on depressive moods have been well documented. In any guide to the illness taking regular exercise is one of the first action points offered to the sufferer. But how can you take exercise three times a week if you can't even get out of bed?

While fighting off a bout of depression in Oxford in the 1980s I decided that I would be all right if only I joined a trendy gym and transformed myself into a muscular sylph. I should have been warned off by the kind of girl I saw in the changing room, but I was still into self-deception at that stage. They were be-thonged and putting on make-up *before* going into an aerobics class! I lied at my fitness test, saying I didn't drink or smoke and was duly given an exercise routine. The first and only time I worked out I found that the goddesses in the gym didn't want to swear or laugh as they exercised. They weren't into solidarity of suffering or chat. In fact, they all looked away into the middle distance, at their cool reflections in the mirrors. They talked only to the fitness instructors, who would lean nonchalantly on their exercise bikes. In my sweats and huge T-shirt I now felt humiliated as well as depressed.

My GP tried to get the hundreds of pounds I'd spent on membership back for me with a medical note, but people like me are the profit margins of these gyms – sad cases who pay for the fantasy, but never turn up to use the resources. Of course, taking exercise when you're depressed can only be helpful. But deciding to join a trendy gym in that state is more than likely to leave you unfit and broke, rather than just unfit, which is what you were before.

3 Don't push yourself to do anything

Moral advice will be of no help to you in a depressed state. In fact, get rid of any moral judgements of yourself whatever, such as 'I'm depressed, therefore I must be a wicked person' or 'I didn't go out, I'm a wimp'. This tendency to make extreme judgements about the self is, in fact, one of depression's symptoms. Your state doesn't mean anything other than that you're ill. Berating yourself in this condition is both useless and mentally cruel. Don't do it to yourself. Give in.

When you're down, the safest place to be is low, because there's nowhere for you to fall.

4 Don't make any decisions while you're depressed

It's one of the illusions of depression that, at last, you're seeing life as it is, stripped of its frills, so now you can make the drastic resolutions that seem to be required in the circumstances. My advice is to do nothing in this state. You'll see why when I tell you that decisions I have taken when low have included:

1. Leaving someone.
2. Staying with the same person.

3. Running away to Brazil.
4. Going blonde (scuppered by my hairdresser, who refused to do it without a doctor's note confirming that I was of sound mind).
5. Training as a radio operator on board a Scandinavian tanker and going to sea.
6. Taking the veil.
7. Growing potatoes in the Scottish Highlands.
8. Baking my own bread and wearing a brown skirt.
9. All of the above.

There may be an element of reality to many of your resolutions, but depression is not so much a disease of *what* you want as *how* you want it.

There will be plenty of time to become a nun when you're feeling more cheerful.

5 Don't forget that all that goes up must come down

There are no free highs in nature. Alcohol is a depressant that looks like a stimulant and will give you a brief high then a kick in the teeth if you're depressed. Chocolate gives you a discernible lift but, when the high wears off, leaves me feeling worse than when I started. Bananas seem to have a beneficial effect on mood, as do avocados, pasta and tomatoes, but I'm told that the blood-brain barrier means that food can't act directly on brain chemistry. If it did I'd eat nothing but bananas.

6 Don't tolerate people who pull you down

The people I mean are those who look like friends but who, somehow or other, always make you feel worse about yourself. They're the ones who discourage you but say it's 'because they care', who spot the flaw in the otherwise perfectly decorated room, who make you feel guilty about being happy and who never seem to know why you're upset after they've told you to pull up your socks.

These people are 'hooks'. They've embedded themselves into you; they use but never give anything back. They let you get away from them so far and then they reel you back in. Some people don't look like hooks but they are. Learn to recognise them all. Straighten them out, each and every one. And if they come at you again, Deploy shields: put on the answer machine, change the locks, call the police, do anything you have to to keep them away.

7 Don't even think about how you are every day

Nothing you do can change the way you feel when you're profoundly depressed, so answering the question 'How are you?' every day is pointless and will, more than likely, make you feel worse. This doesn't mean that you might not improve during the day, but you can take that as a bonus. It's the attempt to measure your wellbeing that's the problem, not the condition itself because the former implies judgement and a falling short of the healthy norm. Refusing to assess yourself gets rid of the guilt you feel about being a drag on your family. It also allows you to get on with your day as it is, without wishing it away. Do your best to be present in your life, however it is at any given point. Think of your illness as no more than the current weather conditions in your area. You're not living in this climate permanently, it's just a passing, freak season. After all, who said you can't enjoy a typhoon, even if it does knock you off your feet?

8 Don't compare yourself with anyone else

Most especially, don't compare yourself to yourself when fit. That 'was in another country and, besides, the wench is dead.'

Depression is awful because it changes you from the person you used to be into someone you don't recognise. But that is also its point. Don't undo its good work by using your old standards. Throw them away because they don't work, or you wouldn't have become so ill in the first place.

9 Don't wish your depression away

Treat it like a bout of malaria, a condition outside the way you normally are. Put on your pyjamas, settle in front of the TV for a night in, ready to ride out the fever for however long it persists.

The last thing you should do is waste your depression. Please don't let all that suffering go to waste. It will give you better clues about the way you're living your life and how right that is for you than anything else. Survived, and used properly, depression could be the best thing that ever happened to you. People who ignore their depression are the ones who go mad, not those who go through it and treat it with the respect it deserves.

10 Don't let depression stop you from enjoying yourself

Your world has collapsed, you're weak as a floor cloth, your morale is in a thousand pieces and yet . . . You see a shadow on the wall you didn't notice before and it's beautiful. Someone cooks risotto and the smell of the rice is so virtuous it makes you want to cry with gratitude. *Enter the Dragon* is shown on TV late at night and it's just what you wanted to see, even though you thought you hated kung-fu.

I know it's not a bundle of laughs, but you can live this out richly and well. Just because you're depressed doesn't mean that you have to be down!

CHAPTER FOUR

My Life as a Ghost

After I'd died of depression, I was quite put out when nobody seemed to have noticed that I'd gone. The boss. My parents. Other than that I was, obviously, replaceable and not nearly as important to other people as I'd thought.

Ghosts see things from another perspective and soon after my hurt pride had settled down, I began to realise that the people from whom I had expected attention were the least able or likely to give it because they were as caught up in their own affairs as I had been before my death.

There were bonuses though, as some completely unexpected people sent cards or phoned and I even ended up making new friends while I was in the grip of clinical depression. These were people who weren't put off by despair knowing, perhaps, something about it themselves. They knew when to send flowers, when to shut up; that a silly card was worth far more than a routine enquiry.

Don't expect to have the same friends in hell as you do in purgatory.

*

> There is in God (some say)
> A deep, but dazling darkness; As men here
> Say it is late and dusky, because they
> See not all clear;
> O for that night! Where I in Him
> Might live invisible and dim.

Henry Vaughan, 'The Night',
The Complete Poetry of Henry Vaughan, ed. French Fogle
(Norton, New York, 1964), p. 325

Self-help is the last thing a depressive needs. It's like driving into fog. Instinctively, you put the headlights on high beam, only to end up confusing yourself even more as the damp air reflects your attempts to see back onto yourself. In this case, if you dare, the safest option is to turn off your headlights altogether and navigate in the dark.

Whoever said we needed light to see?

After three weeks the anti-depressants began to kick in. These affected the quality of my depression but without changing its nature. What they gave me was some psychic space, a small but crucial distance between me and the horrors. Like a line of crustacean riot police, they pushed back the night-mares clamouring for my attention. This gave me a narrow cordon sanitaire in which to move, some room to breathe. The mental crowds were still there, of course, but they had less power over me, as if the anarchists had turned into paparazzi. The lightning of intrusive cameras was blinding, but at least I was free to move out of their way and into sleep's foyer.

It was exactly like when you're being tailgated at night by someone who has their headlights on high beam. You're on a narrow rural road so you can't let them pass, (he's local and knows every twist in the road), so you flip the anti-glare device in your rear-view mirror. The bully depression hasn't gone, he's willing you to turn off or drive more quickly than is safe, but the edge has been taken off his main weapon – light.

> Thinking that their secret sins might escape detec-
> tion beneath a dark pall of oblivion, they lay in
> disorder, dreadfully afraid, terrified by apparitions.
> Not even the dark corner that hid them offered ref-
> uge from fear, but loud, unnerving noises resounded
> about them, and phantoms with faces grim and
> downcast passed before their eyes. No fire, however
> intense, was strong enough to give them light, nor
> were the brilliant, flaming stars adequate to pierce

that hideous darkness. There shone on them only a terrifying blaze of no human making, and in their panic they thought the real world even worse than the sight their imagination conjured up . . .

So all that night, which really had no power over them because it came upon them from the powerless depths of hell, they slept the same haunted sleep, now harried by portentous spectres, now paralysed by the treachery of their own souls . . . The whole world was bathed in the bright light of day, and went about its tasks unimpeded; those people alone were overspread with heavy night, fit image of the darkness that awaited them. But heavier than the darkness was the burden each was to himself.

The Wisdom of Solomon, Chapter 17: 3–6, 14–16, 20
The Apocrypha, *The Revised English Bible*

If I tried to get up of my own accord, I would be hit down by an onslaught of chaotic energy, which literally knocked me off my feet.

At these times I learnt that it was best to play dead. Despite rising panic in my throat, I'd lie as still as I possibly could, keeping my mind firmly gagged as I felt a wild presence snuffle around me, looking for any purchase, a weak spot. Stifling the impulse to run I'd listen to this bear's stale breath testing my being (expecting to feel its claws tearing me to pieces any second). Eventually, disappointed by the dead meat it had found, this intelligence gradually moved away, its interest in me distracted by more promising kill.

> Surgeons from four cities travelled to Derbyshire Royal Infirmary for eight 'spare part organs' from a donor, it was disclosed yesterday.
>
> The operations were carried out in three hours by nine surgeons at the weekend.
>
> Two doctors travelled from Papworth Hospital, Cambridge, for the heart and lungs, and three from Queen Elizabeth Hospital, Birmingham for the liver.
>
> Two surgeons drove from the City Hospital, Nottingham, to take the kidneys and two doctors from the Derbyshire Royal Infirmary's ophthalmic unit recovered the corneas . . .
>
> In the present state of medical knowledge there is not much more that could have been donated when death was declared.
>
> *The Times*, 26 January, 1987

*

I noticed how I never used my shoes any more and wondered if my feet would ever fit into my RM Williams boots again after I'd been barefoot in bed for so long.

My mother said, tactlessly, 'You won't be getting any wear out of those nice suits you bought for work. What a waste'. For all I cared Leighton could have cleared out my wardrobe and given my clothes away to charity. I had no use for my old things nor my old life. If I ever started living again, I wouldn't even recognise myself.

This is how Zen describes poverty of spirit: being so bereft of personality that, even if you wanted to hang yourself you couldn't find a self to hang.

I'd already abandoned my public self, my existence within the family, any semblance of being a writer. Instinctively, I wanted to hold on to the little I had left – ideas, values, a personal mythology. But something told me that possessiveness wasn't the antidote to this particular stripping down. Perhaps what was needed was losing far more.

I was ready to be a corpse for as long it took. Ready to listen.

> In life, you see, there is not much choice. You have either to rot or to burn. And there is not one of us, painted or unpainted, that would not rather burn than rot.
>
> Joseph Conrad, *Under Western Eyes*, (OUP, 1983), p. 250

*

When women were condemned to be burned as witches, it's said that those who really cared for their relatives didn't come to the last visit with tears and grief. This wasn't a time for sentiment. They brought the women flax to tie around their bodies, so that they might burn more quickly.

> You must be ready to burn yourself in
> your own flame: how could you become new, if
> you had not first become ashes?
>
> Nietzsche, *Thus Spoke Zarathustra*,
> tr RJ Hollingdale (Penguin, 1961), p. 90

My favourite painter in the National Museum of Wales in Cardiff, which has a wonderful collection of Impressionist art, is Eugène Carrière. He's not blockbuster-famous, like Monet, but was known to the painters and writers of his time. He was the founder of the Société Nationale des Beaux Arts, was an important influence on Gauguin and his students included Matisse and Derain. I think of him as the Dark Impressionist.

His pictures in Cardiff are portraits of mothers with babies, all painted with a sepia and peat palette. Out of the surrounding dark the tissue-thin skin of a baby stretched over the soft cranium has a horribly fragile sheen to it; you can pick out the glow of a pewter cup, the glint of the mother's wedding ring. Carrière's babies are no bouncing cherubs, they're unbearably close to sickness and death.

This was a man who saw life through the dark. Living bodies are the temporary exception to shadows and we feel they won't last long nor live in joy. Carrière made colour seem vulgar because he dared ask the question: If you give up colour what can be left of light?

Carrière's family groupings convey the dream-like pain of losing, with the dull ache that blocks out detail. In one Musée d'Orsay canvas, *The Sick Child*, the family group is feverishly diffuse, as if the painter shared the infant's delirium. The only thing in focus is the piercing gaze of the dying baby. What he sees most clearly is what we know will soon disappear, whereas objects which catch the light – a porcelain bowl, a glass – will outlive their users.

In another painting, *Baiser Maternelle*, the mother's kiss is so ardent that it seems to devour the face of the child she loves. Its soft skull melts like wax in fire, buckles under her ardour. The child can't escape this love and it sucks the life out of it, leaving its orbital sockets empty of eyes. These Carrière women and children are hungry ghosts.

*

Some mornings I would feel like myself for ten minutes, only to come crashing down again, my morale a pile of dust.

Bewildered, I'd look around the room and would be almost scared by how solid the furniture seemed, how assertive the wallpaper. The folds in the curtains had authority, an ease in the light that I couldn't feel myself. That was the problem: I'd lost all sense of myself.

I swear that if I'd tried to move a lamp, my hand would have gone straight through it.

By now it was becoming clear even to me that I wasn't going to be back in work in a couple of days' time. I stopped berating myself for malingering and I relaxed into the experience of depression.

Most of my days were still spent sleeping, but there were short periods of consciousness between the heavy-duty oblivion into which I could slip any time of the day or night. One of the classic symptoms of depression is sleep disruption, which usually means waking up early or being unable to sleep when you're exhausted. My problem was the opposite: I couldn't wake up. I gorged myself like a teenager on sleep and still felt worn out. Sitting at our dining table was as tiring as strenuous exercise. Reading the paper was out of the question.

This virulent somnolence makes me think of Sleeping

Beauty. The direct result of a curse, the princess falls asleep and a forest of thorns grows up around her through which the prince has to fight his way to wake her. Now I think that the wicked step mother's spell might not have been as malign as it appeared, and that the forest might have sprung up to protect Sleeping Beauty, to keep her asleep until she was ready to face the world.

Bernadette said to the other sisters, 'I shall continue my work.'
   'What work, Bernadette?'
   'Being ill.'

Hugo Claus, *The Sorrow of Belgium*

Propped up on my pillows, in bed, I could see Waterloo Road outside, the pavement and one long red-brick wall. When I was awake enough to be upright, I'd look out at the weather, at people scurrying to work or to the shops and the garbage vans removing the rubbish. I listened so often to the morning and evening rush hours going past our bedroom window that I learned the exact tuning of local buses, how the school coaches took the corner, the precise attack with which the 3.20 pm bus from town addressed the hill on which we live.

It was a rainy, much moaned-about winter, but it seemed beautiful to me, especially when the sun turned the wet road silver and people's shadows followed them, their darkness at 90 degrees to their animated figures along the shining wall.

> I'm saving Virginia Woolf for when
> I'm dead.
>
> Julian Barnes, *Flaubert's Parrot*,
> (Picador, London, 1984), p. 109

Taking part in a Zen retreat is like having a homeopathic dose of death. You wear black in order not to draw your fellow-sitters' eyes unnecessarily. The retreat is silent, so you don't chat, read, listen to the radio, or pull yourself out of the act of internal recollection to which you've made a commitment. There's no need to choose when to do anything, a routine is laid down: up at 6 am, lights out at 9.30 pm. The food is good and meals are eaten at regular intervals;

there are even chocolate biscuits for tea. I love this discipline because its purpose isn't prohibitive but to give you maximum inner freedom. It gets rid of distractions so that you can get on with looking at what you've come to see.

Inside is not always a pretty picture. Charged with the task of concentrating only on your breath and letting everything else die away, your mind is like a washing machine in overdrive and very far from the civilised entity you had assumed it was. You think of lists of things you haven't done, incidents from your schooldays flash before you and you're sure that the shooting pain in your head is a brain tumour. It's humiliating to find you can't even go one second without following the conscious mind's phantasmagoria. I had thought that Zen was meant to lead to peace of mind, but I found myself in the half-lotus position at the end of one session outwardly serene but screaming inside for the leader to hit the bronze bowl to mark the start of the break: 'Ring the bell, goddamit. Ring the fucking bell!!!'.

If you can shift your attention from your thoughts' whirligig for more than two seconds, however, something miraculous happens. You fail hundreds of times, but stubbornly bring yourself back again. You think of yourself as a fish in a river; if you want to stay alive you have to resist the bait offered by your own mind. And eventually the uproar recedes, you mind it less, you become tolerant of it but not swept up in its childishness. ('I must grab a banana at lunchtime. I hope they're not all gone. I really fancy a banana.')

My first retreat I knew that I'd embarked on my biggest adventure ever. I've travelled plenty, but I'd never gone as far as I might because I hadn't dared to make the journey of staying still.

What I'd found was shocking: my mind a cross between a terrorist and a clown, throwing itself around, ready to do anything to keep my own attention. I'd suspected I was a bit off-centre, but now I had proof that my body was nothing more than a bespoke straitjacket.

Somehow I sensed that, in its infinite self-tolerance, I might have found a long-term solution in Zen to depression. If daily dying was what it took, then I was ready to do it.

Obsession

1 The action of besieging . . .

2 The hostile action of the devil or an evil spirit besetting anyone; actuation by the devil or an evil spirit from without; the fact of being thus beset or actuated.

3 *(transf.)* The action of any influence, notion, or 'fixed idea', which persistently assails or vexes, especially so as to discompose the mind.

The Compact Edition of the Oxford English Dictionary, Vol I
(Oxford University Press, 1971)

When Mary Magdalene was exorcised by Christ, it's said that seven demons came out of her. Much of what the past called evil spirits we now recognise as the symptoms of mental illness. Mary Magdalene's 'fixed ideas' were her ghosts and Christ, like a psychiatrist, freed her of them.

Ghosts are dead stories of which we refuse to let go.

This is what my ghosts were telling me:

'I told you you shouldn't listen to yourself. You should never have tried to be a writer, but should have gone into the civil service, like I wanted you to. You've broken my heart by being a failure, despite all my sacrifices. If you'd been any kind of person at all, you'd have tried above all to make your mother happy.'

'Nothing you touch will ever go well, because you bought it at other people's cost. Now pay the price for your selfishness.'

These messages never changed, except that my ghosts became more skilful at speaking to maximum effect – whenever I had begun to hope that I might recover from the past, or when I was feeling vulnerable.

I felt possessed.

> In the State of Possession, the victims of psychic and physical invaders becomes auto-allergic, re-acting against the body's own tissues, the spirit's own processes.
>
> Noam Chomsky

*

I had made my ghosts so welcome in my life that I no longer knew who was real and who was dead. What they were saying had long ago lost connection with the actual people in my experience and had become internal caricatures, with a destructive life of their own. What had started as a particular history had changed in my head to a crippling judgmentalism, self-criticism run riot. Sitting still for five days showed me clearly the violence of this habit of mine and what I'd been doing to myself.

A ghost is always a forgery of some kind, based on only one side of the story between people. This is why they're dangerous company and can lead to living a falsified life, as they serve an egotistic agenda that refuses to be changed. Ghosts are ultimately boring because their lives are never real.

I decided to open a door and let my ghouls do what they wanted. After all, ghosts are only alarming if you're afraid of them.

The famous healer Lilla Bek has a story about a woman who went to live in a haunted house. The ghost used to appear at the foot of her bed each night. Instead of being afraid, the woman used to look at the apparition and say 'Oh, hello again, dear. I'm off to sleep now, but please make yourself at home if you want to. Whatever you choose to do is fine and isn't going to bother me.' After three months or so the ghost's appearance began to change and one night a beautiful spectral man thanked her and disappeared. That was the last time the ghost visited her. Because the woman had refused to be frightened by the original apparition, it was able to complete the work it had to do in her house and find the peace it wanted.

(Recounted in Lilla Bek, Philippa Pullar,
The Seven Levels of Healing (Rider, 1987), p. 128

> But you yourself will always be the worst enemy you
> can encounter; you yourself lie in wait for yourself
> in caves and forests.
>
> Nietzsche, *Thus Spoke Zarathustra*, p. 90

My father is the son of a miner and grandson of the Methodist minister who led the 1904 Revival in Ogmore Vale, South Wales. He's a deacon in his chapel but, theologically, he has a very unconventional mind. He once showed me some notes on Buddhism he'd made forty years ago, so maybe I inherited my spiritual curiosity from him.

He surprised me recently by lending me a book on spiritualism. He explained that, when he was a student public health officer in the Isle of Sheppey just after the war, he'd lodged with an established Spiritualist family and had been invited to their services. He wasn't attracted by the prospect of talking to the departed but he did respect the integrity of the family's gift for discerning spirits. He believes in the spirit world himself but without feeling the need to see a ghost. He's humble enough to live with faith rather than requiring proof.

I enjoyed the book he lent me, when I could read again. It was written by Aelwyn Roberts, a Church in Wales vicar who's a licensed exorcist. He works with Elwyn Roberts, a poet and medium and the book contains quite a few traditional ghost stories, mysteries solved, presences soothed.

But what struck me most of all was Aelwyn Roberts's description of the way in which his friend speaks to ghosts: 'No, don't go, love. Stay with us. It was you I came here to see.' (Aelwyn Roberts, *Pobol Ddoe* ('Yesterday's People') (Gwasg Gee, 1997), p. 14). Rather than screaming at them to leave me alone, might this be another, better, way for me to talk to my ghosts?

You don't need permission from a ghost to live. It's he or she who needs permission from the living to die.

When you are used by your thoughts, your feet are
not planted firmly on the ground, in fact you have
no feet at all. You are only the shadow of a human

being, blown about by circumstances . . . You there,
with the wind whistling through your nightie, what
is your original self?

Robert Aitken, *Taking the Path of Zen*,
(North Point Press, San Francisco, 1982) p. 100

The reason I wanted to study Zen was that I no longer wanted
to live like a ghost, but to feel the present fully.

Far from being an airy-fairy discipline, Zen's precepts are
spectacularly down-to-earth. 'Zen has nothing to do with
nihilism', the Japanese Roshi told us one time. 'You are here
to ask the life-and-death question: Who am I?'

Sister Elaine explained that Zen Buddhists see the self as
a monolith. All energy comes from the Buddha nature, or
larger mind, which is the infinite. This energy goes wherever
we want it to. Our conscious, or narrow minds – which is
what we use to imagine, feel, remember, project – all our
ego activities need energy to operate and this is our normal
mode of being. Like boulders in a river, these activities
impede the energy current, but are worn down slowly by the
flow, until the Buddha nature eventually breaks through.
Then the Buddha nature, unimpeded by the ego, is able to
use its power in its own way.

For the first time I understood why conscious thought
needs to be stopped in meditation. If the whole self is busy
plotting, or remembering, the energy isn't being directed

towards breaking down old complexes, fears and blocks. In meditation this energy first has a therapeutic effect and then leads to spiritual experience. My assumption had always been that it was somehow morally better not to focus on the chatter in your mind, but it had never before been explained to me that the energy which that used could be better employed in bypassing those processes altogether and living from a larger, less deluded place in the self.

The point of Zen isn't to make you feel better but to allow you to see where you are in reality. Live in that reality and no ghost can ever touch you again.

A lion was taken into captivity and thrown into a concentration camp where, to his amazement, he found other lions who had been there for years, some of them all their lives, for they had been born there. He soon became acquainted with the social activities of the camp lions. They banded themselves into groups. One group consisted of the socializers; another was into show business; another was cultural, for its purpose was to carefully preserve the customs, the tradition, the history of the times when lions were free; other groups were religious – they gathered mostly to sing moving songs about a future jungle where there would be no fences; some groups attracted those who were

literary and artistic by nature; others still were revolutionary, and they met to plot against their captors
or against other revolutionary groups. Every now
and then a revolution would break out, one particular group would be wiped out by another, or the
guards would all be killed and replaced by another
set of guards.

As he looked around, the newcomer observed one
lion who always seemed deep in thought, a loner
who belonged to no group and mostly kept away
from everyone. There was something strange about
him that commanded everyone's admiration and
everyone's hostility, for his presence aroused fear
and self-doubt. He said to the newcomer, 'Join no
group. These poor fools are busy with everything
except what is essential.'

'And what is that?'

'Studying the nature of the fence.'

Anthony de Mello, *The Heart of the Enlightened*,
(Fount, 1989), pp. 184–85

Once a friend told me this old Welsh story. A young man
was in trouble and made a pact with a magician. The deal
was that he would have his heart's desire if he could stay on
top of the mountain three nights running. The magician told
him that all he had to do to be safe was to stand his ground,
that nothing could hurt him as long as he stayed within the
magic circle that had been drawn around him.

The first night the young boy was assailed by a horde of
ghosts who charged at him like cavalry. He remembered the
magician's words and stood still and the ghouls went right
past him. The second night the demons attacked in a storm

of thunder and lightning the like of which had never been seen before. The boy was frightened but he stood his ground and the dangerous weather passed over him, leaving him unharmed.

The third night he was feeling pretty pleased with himself and already enjoying his wish in his mind. Suddenly a huge wheel of fire rolled towards him through the bracken. Instinctively, he jumped out of its way and – before he knew it – out of the magic circle. In the morning he was found dead.

In my sickbed I decided to give up any control at all over my thoughts and let whatever wanted to come, without judging it at all.

Instead, I began to listen to my own breathing, and found it strangely soothing. Aside from the light, and the chaos in my head, it was the main thing going on in the room. It was beyond my conscious control and seemed to be tougher and bigger than myself. I held on to it, and let the thoughts rush past me. Often, this had the effect of soothing me to sleep, much better than the ridiculous ghost ride going on in my mind.

I was learning to stand my ground.

There was an old gentleman in our neighbourhood who always seemed to be waiting for a bus. He was about ninety, bone-thin, but immaculately dressed in shirt and tie, his shoes polished, a raincoat over his three-piece suit, hair neatly cut and a hat on his head. He was curved like a question mark and greeted all the passers-by – schoolgirls, the window cleaner, dog-walkers. Leighton and I began to notice, though, that however many buses went by, he never seemed to get on any of them. He'd let them go and continue waiting, as if that were the main task of his day. One month he'd obviously had a fall and he'd inch along the pavement on a zimmer frame, but still well turned out.

The quality of this man's waiting – he was out in the day, no matter what – was more important than any bus that he could catch.

The problem with censorship is that it's never selective enough: it always ends up blocking out the valuable with the pernicious. The endless battle of judgmental voices in my head had caused me so much pain that I'd go to great lengths to suppress them. But the casualty of such fear was that I had also blocked out my own truthful voices, so that I didn't know where the hell I was or what I thought of anything.

Because I was incapable of doing anything now, I began to learn that, however many thought buses came past my bed, I didn't have to catch any of them. I began to let the buses go by, just watching them.

This was the single most important thing I learnt in this bout of depression. It seems like nothing, but its effects were huge. Ghosts can't harm you, and neither can depression – unless you believe they can.

*

Amongst other things, ghosts are energy thieves. I'm talking now about those living ghosts who always seem to drain you dry, leaving you exhausted after an encounter. They're people who trap you in their company, who know how to make you stay much longer than you had planned and feel guilty about leaving. Then, breathless, you sit in the car outside and want to scream because they've sucked the life out of you, against your will.

These are people who refuse to pay their own energy bills. They tap into the nearest lamppost or next door's electricity supply (that means yours) and use it liberally. When you bring up the matter of your latest crippling bill, they look offended and you end up apologising to them for being mean-spirited.

You must avoid these people at all costs if you're depressed, even if they're closely related to you. You're half-dead already and, in this state, meeting an energy incubus might finish you off altogether.

> I am now making a strong effort to discipline myself against the obsession with this and other wasteful family problems that have robbed me of my vitality during the last twelve years – unmanned me time and again and threatened to make me one of those emotional derelicts who are nothing but tremulous jellyfish might-have-beens.
>
> Hart Crane, 1928, Quoted in John Unterecker,
> *Voyager: A Life of Hart Crane* (Anthony Blond, 1970), p. 565

*

I didn't notice at the time, but Leighton was always at home when I woke up. Much later, I found out that he'd seriously neglected his business in order to be in the house. I told him that I didn't feel suicidal and, even if I did, I didn't have enough energy to hurt myself. Secretly I was glad that he had taken matters into his own hands.

Leighton also gave me the best present I've ever had, in the depths of my doldrums. He came home one day with a winter-flowering cherry tree. The lady in the garden centre had advised him to take not the flashiest plant but a more delicate tree that she felt sure would grow especially beautifully. With me watching from the bedroom window, we picked the right spot at the side of the house and he pulled up a paving stone, bedded the tree in soil and fed it.

A winter-flowering tree is the perfect gift for a depressive. It's an act of faith that something will stir in the dark. It says: it doesn't matter if you're out of season compared to the rest of the world, everything blossoms in its own time, and midwinter can be fruitful.

Despair in this case is not merely passive suffering but action. For when the earthly is taken away from the self and a man despairs, it is as if despair came from without, though it comes nevertheless always from the self . . . For just because this despair is

more intense, salvation is in a certain sense nearer.
Such a despair will hardly forget, it is too deep; but
despair is held open every instant, and there is thus
possibility of salvation.

Søren Kierkegaard, 'The Sickness Unto Death'
in *Fear and Trembling and The Sickness Unto
Death*, tr Walter Lowrie (Doubleday Anchor Books,
New York, 1951), p. 196

In the steadily hardening light of late January, the world was,
indeed, getting on with its business. A combative Italian
neighbour caused a scandal in our respectable Edwardian
street (tessellated floors, Many Original Features) by painting
his whole house, bricks and all, orange. The neighbours were
furious and I would often hear raised voices from the street
as a cowboy builder Tangoed the house. There was muttering
about planning permission, thousands being knocked off the
value of our houses. He even painted the inside orange. Was
it a job-lot of paint, I wonder?

Orange is the colour of madness, they say, but I kind of
liked it.

*

If you'd asked me during this period I'd have said I was very happy. I was suffering, of course, but that's something different.

My worst nightmare had happened: I had been stripped down by depression into being an invalid. It was humiliating, losing everything that I thought fetching about myself – my humour, my distinctive point of view, even my usual smell. And yet, I was able to endure and still felt human. Even though I didn't recognise myself, in some ways I was already, even in this pitiful state, feeling better than I had before I became ill.

Something important was changing in the dark inside me. Lethargy isn't the opposite of energy, but its predecessor. I felt like a computer that was trying to catch up with itself, swallowing new information, discarding the old.

People in the middle of depression are beings who have to live, for a while, without a story, which is why it feels as though you've lost your soul. But this period is a dark room where you're developing the next chapter of your life before living it. The work will be all the more vivid if you're patient and let it take its own course.

Each morning I'd look at the cherry tree outside, waiting for the first frost-coaxed blossom to appear.

*

Study me, then, you who shall lovers bee
At the next world, that is, at the next Spring:
      For I am every dead thing,
      In whom love wrought new Alchemy.
        For his art did expresse
A quintessence even from nothingnesse,
From dull privations, and leane emptinesse:
He ruin'd me, and I am re-begot
Of absence, darknesse, death; things which are not.

John Donne, 'A Nocturnall Upon S. Lucies Day, Being The Shortest Day',
John Donne: Complete Poetry and Selected Prose,
ed. John Hayward (The Nonesuch Press, 1990), p. 32

It was nearly midwinter in 1993 when Leighton and I were married. We figured that if we could be happy at the darkest time of year, nothing could touch us.

On Christmas Day the cherry tree blossomed. Later, as the light grew stronger and I was able to move around I noticed in rain a second, lighter tree lying on the branches of the first – crystal and closer than its shadow, which circled the blossoming tree like a ghost.

*

Peredur rode on towards a river valley whose edges were forested, with level meadows on both sides of the river; on one bank there was a flock of white sheep, and on the other a flock of black sheep. When a white sheep bleated a black sheep would cross the river and turn white, and when a black sheep bleated a white sheep would cross the river and turn black. On the bank of the river he saw a tall tree: from roots to crown one half was aflame and the other green with leaves.

The Mabinogion, tr. Jeffrey Gantz (Penguin, 1976), p. 243

CHAPTER FIVE

Portrait of a Missing Person

Someone once told me about a newspaper story claiming that all left-handed people were the single survivors of a pair of twins, one of whom had been lost very early in pregnancy. If this is true, why not think of all of us single offspring as the lost half of a pair of twins? It would explain our terrible loneliness, the sense of something missing, our homesickness for ourselves.

When, after finishing my degree in 1982, I went to America I felt that I'd entered a parallel universe. This continent had weather, mornings, light but no sign of my previous existence. I sometimes felt that I was lacking my own twin, my shadow.

I missed rain and found the choice of butter in the supermarkets overwhelming. The students in Harvard were physically very fit, but the conformism of their casual clothes made me want to rebel and wear suits, Edwardian lace-up boots and hats. Most of all, I missed speaking Welsh although I did discover that the Wiedener Library in Harvard Yard had a good collection of Welsh poetry.

I spent my year in Harvard reading widely, eating, learning German and trying to write. One day I saw Seamus Heaney in the library. I knew he was teaching a poetry workshop, so I edged up to him, took my courage in both hands, and asked if I could take part. He agreed, so I was lucky enough to attend the good-humoured sessions he ran, combining perceptive points about literature with jokes and anecdotes. I never dared show him any of my work.

Through mutual friends I began teaching Welsh to a woman we knew as Wendy the Witch. She was a very kind, blonde bombshell from Salem and she gave me tarot readings instead of money for the lessons. Later, she even agreed to teach me how to read the Aleister Crowley deck. Wendy used the cards as a way of analysing the current situation in your life through archetypal images, rather than in any occult way, and that made a great deal of sense to me. I began to use the cards as a way of looking at problems which were blocking my way forward.

Somehow or other, that year, I came across Goya's *Caprichos*, a series of etchings by the nineteenth-century Spanish painter. The most famous of these shows a man dreaming with the epitaph 'The sleep of reason brings forth monsters'. In his *Caprichos*, a surreal satire on post French-Revolution Spain, Goya portrayed a bizarre world of animals as judges and priests, old hags pulling teeth out of the mouths of men hung on gibbets, women who are half-bird procuring young girls for soldiers. I was so fascinated by these etchings that I made large black-and-white photocopies of them and pinned them in different sequences all around my room, as though they were tarot cards and could tell a story.

The etching that disturbed me most showed a woman being carried away by two stooped, hooded figures. The captor on the left is swathed in a sheet or in a monk's habit. We can't see his face at all. In the shadows we can pick out the sturdy legs of the second man, who holds the woman in an erotic embrace around her waist. He has a scarf around his head and instead of a face there is darkness.

The woman flings her head back with sexual abandon, so that the moonlight or streetlight from above shows us every contorted detail of her features, her hair falling down behind her, as if in water. She's screaming, yes, but it's the silent scream of nightmares and there's a suggestion of collusion in her capture in the way her legs aren't kicking but her feet are set formally together, heel-to-heel, as if she were about to begin dancing. The subtitle reads drily: 'Que se la Llevaron' ('They carried her off'). The woman who doesn't take care of herself will be carried away. You just know that this woman will never be seen again.

This *Capricho* chilled me to the bone. As a parable of the self-abandonment that has to happen before you cast yourself in the role of victim, it scared me to death. I already knew that I found inhabiting my own skin very uncomfortable, and that I could easily be carried away by other people. In the sensuality of this woman's self-loss, I saw the possibility of this habit turning into a compulsion, something akin to an addiction. I put the other etchings away but left this one up on my wall, perhaps as a warning.

The kind of depression from which I suffer doesn't come

out of nowhere. It's like a rare plant that needs certain soil conditions to root, a specific period of darkness and then a very precise sequence of temperatures to allow it to germinate. Three factors – genetics, habit and crisis – need to be present for this dark flower to blossom. Aside from a genetic predisposition towards depression, I can now pick out some long-term emotional habits which made it increasingly likely, looking back, that a crisis in the short-term would flip over into clinical depression.

Nobody can change their genetic disposition, but depressive habits of mind are shiftable, even if they're buried deep in your personal history. This is what shrinks and psychotherapists are for, to help you disentangle the 'given facts' of your life (things you can't change) from the choices you've made in your reactions to these facts (things you can change). In this chapter I want to look at the growth of those deep emotional habits which, I think, made me prone to the depression, to which I already had a genetic tendency. It's taken me many years to understand them myself. This is where the hardest slog of detective work comes in – a determined sifting of old history, painful events, those experiences you would do almost anything to avoid looking at. Except now you're desperate and face a worse enemy: depression.

Knowledge of this kind gives you power to choose how you react and a fighting chance against that terrible cloud. And for that, it's worth it.

*

After a year I found Harvard suffocating so I applied to move to Columbia University, in New York. I must be the only person to have been admitted to the Graduate Writing programme there by showing poems written originally in Welsh. These were scribbled frantically in a couple of days, under the pressure of having to submit work to apply for a place. The one thing I knew when I moved down to New York was that I had, at all costs, to begin writing poetry in English, though I couldn't imagine how I was going to overcome my loyalty to Welsh.

I found a place to live in So-ho in the traditional Welsh way – by talking to someone on the street – and, just before term started, moved into a walk-up railroad apartment with a shower in the kitchen. Andy Warhol lived in Spring Street, just round the corner, and I used to see his strange matt grey hair often, though I never spoke to him. I knew some artists who lived in a loft nearby but, other than that, I was totally alone.

One evening we were in our favourite bar, Fenelli's, when someone asked me if it was true I was a poet. I hummed and ha'd and the person (an artist himself) asked me again: 'This is really important. You have to decide. Are you a poet or not?' I took a deep breath, made a choice, and staked my life on it.

'Yes. I'm a poet.'

*

Can you remember a time in your life when nothing, absolutely nothing was decided about who you were or what you might be? At Columbia, I had no idea if I could write again, no inkling of how I was going to build a life, how I was going to earn a living, what my values were or what I was going to discover about myself.

America had always been hospitable to this kind of openness and even encourages self-invention. As I screwed up the courage to change from writing in Welsh to English as well, I needed this kind of support, this willingness to try anything and be unafraid of failure. Because something hadn't been done before was no reason not to do it. Indeed, it was a good reason to do it. People were interested in my knowledge of the Welsh tradition, not contemptuous of it, and didn't see it as a liability in the twentieth century.

One of our teachers at Columbia was the Nobel laureate, Joseph Brodsky. He believed intensely in the importance of poetry in society; back in Russia he had been condemned to five years' internal exile for 'parasitism' and writing 'anti-Soviet' poetry. His seminars were electrifying. He believed that what distinguishes us from other species is speech, and that poetry, as the supreme linguistic operation, is our anthropological, indeed, genetic goal. He wasn't claiming importance for poetry on the romantic grounds of the poet's own personality but on the basis of our mutual genetic and linguistic inheritance. This was the opposite of self-inflation. Indeed, he would often speak ironically in class about 'my humble self' and one of his tests for the greatness of a poet was whether or not he could imagine the world without himself in it.

Brodsky had refused to make his exile from Russia a melo-drama and was determined that it should be 'business as usual' when he came to the United States to live. The personal cost of this move to him was enormous. And yet, he told us, that you have to face the loneliness of being a poet without attempting to blunt it, even if you do have to 'make that long-distance phone call' from time to time.

New York was the loneliest place I'd ever been. Even when I had got to know some fellow students at Columbia quite well, I remember commenting in the Hungarian Coffee House near the university 'You lot are always rushing off. I'm the only one who stays.' This was more than a different social rhythm – everyone else seemed to have family or old friends in the city, as a buffer around them. In such a big city there's no need to work at relationships that don't come easily, to make an effort to resolve conflict, because people are always replaceable. I was somewhat relieved when a journalist friend of mine confided that he'd had a similar experience of New York. He was mentally tougher than I was but commented that in the city you didn't need strangers to screw you because, sometimes, your 'friends' did it for you.

One evening, coming back downtown from Columbia on the subway, I was so lonely that I began to cry. I knew it was dangerous to show vulnerability on the streets, but I didn't care. I no longer felt human. Nobody talked to me, of course, on the subway. I suppose I should have been grateful for that.

At that time, poetry was the only solid land I had, the only way of picking my way into the future. There was very little of it on which I could put my feet, but at least they were still in some kind of contact with the ground.

That ended on the night I was mugged.

New Yorkers seldom invite you to their apartments, because home is the realm that is kept most private, for family and lovers only. However, I was still European enough to want to entertain. With two friends from his poetry seminar at Columbia, I invited Joseph Brodsky to dinner and he accepted.

I bought a tablecloth to cover the brown vinyl of my circular table, and cooked bluefish in foil with lemon juice and onions. I was beside myself with excitement that Joseph had agreed to come. His conversation was heady because he treated us as equals, talked to us as if we were poets. We quizzed him about which American writers he rated, about his life in the Soviet Union and he held forth to us about modernism and a strange story about his intending to hijack a plane in Russia using his black pen as a replica gun. At the airport, he said, he went into a shop, bought a bag of walnuts and knew he couldn't go through with it. He stayed to talk with us till well after midnight, chain smoking, tugging the filters out of his cigarettes with his teeth and spitting them out with contempt.

After he left, my friends and I were still so excited that we couldn't think of going to bed, so we hatched a tipsy plan to go uptown to watch the balloons being inflated for the Macy's Thanksgiving Day Parade, which was to take place the next day. This seemed like a good idea for a while but, by the time we'd made our way up to Central Park, seen a couple of bobbing cartoon characters, we'd sobered up, so we decided to go our separate ways.

By now it was about two o'clock in the morning and I took the subway, which was surprisingly busy for that time of night. The train I boarded stopped unexpectedly at 14th Street and I decided to walk the rest of the way home, rather than risk waiting alone on a platform. I knew, of course, that walking home wasn't a great plan but I was so high after the dinner that I decided that, if I stuck to the main avenues and made sure I was always within sight of other people, I could risk it.

I was nearly home when it happened. As I was walking briskly down the Avenue of the Americas (having placed myself strategically in front of a couple also walking in the same direction) I suddenly felt that something was wrong. I'd just crossed a side street by the dry cleaners and out of the corner of my eye I saw a shadow moving quickly and purposefully towards my own. I was concerned enough to start turning around but before I could do so a man grabbed me from behind. A knife flashed. I pulled my purse out of my pocket but he didn't seem to want that. He was pulling me backwards by my hair and his knife was telling me without words not to scream. The man was shorter than me so I twisted awkwardly as he pulled me away from the orange light of the avenue towards the side street's gloom, where I could sense a patch of waste ground, rusty fire escapes and places where a person could disappear.

Then I heard a shout from the avenue. Incredibly, the couple walking behind me had stopped and, fully lit themselves, were peering into the darkness around us.

Then everything slowed to a mythical pace. As the couple waited, uncertain, on the avenue, the man turned and put his arm around my shoulders, pulling me towards him, like a lover. All the time he kept the knife pressed into my stomach. I could do nothing except wait and pray that the two figures in the light wouldn't be fooled by this pantomime, wouldn't turn and walk on.

One of them crossed the road, but the woman waited, continuing to stare and we were held, frozen in her gaze, poised between life and the underworld. I suddenly realised that I was closer to this man who probably wanted to rape and possibly kill me, than I'd been to anybody else in the city. I started to get really scared.

Then there were two figures again in the sodium light and the woman shouted that they'd called the police. The endless moment poised between two worlds, with the mugger holding on to me so intimately, so easily, snapped shut. I shoved him away and ran towards the light.

Later safely back in my apartment I shook and shook. I called my friends from Columbia but one had her answering machine on. The other said that he couldn't possibly come down because of his girlfriend. Thus, in classic New York style, I'd been mugged twice, once by a stranger and once

by a so-called friend. I spent the night awake with the radio
on and the taps running for comfort.

Something went missing in me after that night. My mother
taught us never to pass someone on the stairs, in case you
inadvertently trade souls. Although he didn't do what he'd
planned, in that moment of perfect poise before he ran his
way and I ran mine, the mugger had taken something of
mine. The event that didn't happen did and although I was
quickly out and about again I knew that a part of myself had
been carried off, like the victim in the Goya etching. I'd failed
to look after myself in the most basic fashion. Perhaps what
I'd learned was that if you wanted to be a poet you had to
give up any hope of a life. No, it was more than that. The
price of writing was abandoning part of yourself that went,
obediently, with your lover, Hades, into the dark.

On a rational level I knew, of course, how lucky I'd been
and that I'd acted very foolishly. From then on, however
strapped I was for cash, I always made sure I had the taxi fare
home at night. I carried on studying at Columbia, finished the
course, and stayed friends with Brodsky, who was always
ready to have lunch. One time we met I felt so homesick
that when he said something kind, I began to cry. His advice
was to take myself off to a cheap hotel in Algeria or Morocco
and to 'look at the distant line of the sea', the last thing I

needed because I was already wretchedly lonely, but he meant well. We walked out to the end of one of the Manhattan piers and looked at the Hudson flowing past. 'Making it in New York is a false promise, you know,' he said. 'You have to do what you really love and your poems will come out of that.' Now I understand what he was telling me, but it took me a very long time to know what he meant and even longer to live it.

When I phoned Wales, they said, 'Cut your losses and come home' but I couldn't because I hadn't done the writing I needed to, in all freedom, away from the people and cultures that I feared would overwhelm me. I knew that if I left before starting that in earnest, I'd never do it back in Britain. So I stuck it out, worked hard, wrote badly but still kept at it, no matter what.

In the meantime my life was getting progressively worse. Once you start throwing yourself away, it becomes easier with practice. To save money on rent I moved from So-ho north to the Upper West Side and into a series of shared apartments. I had less and less money, as I was determined to devote my time to writing rather than earning a good living. At one point I had so little money that I couldn't afford toiletries or to have my glasses repaired when I dropped them and one of the lenses cracked. My clothes were hand-me-downs from a friend's Park Avenue mother – very good quality but a little strange on me. I had plenty of time to do what I wanted. I'd often walk over to the Metropolitan Museum and, instead of learning about art chronologically, I'd have theme days: one afternoon I'd look only at Breasts, another Beards, or Ships. I started to ride a bicycle around Manhattan to save on subway fares. This is fine for lean lycraed messengers with racing bikes and helmets, but a slow form of suicide on a sit-up-and-beg bike, wearing a skirt.

I learnt to drink gin street-style (no tonic, with a bite of lemon) and drank a lot. Poverty saps the morale in ways you don't notice because it happens gradually. Soon I was living on nothing but broccoli, rice and Parmesan; my German landlady ordered me to wash the sheets on my bed. And still I sat for hours in the noisy apartment (wax ear plugs in) trying to write.

I cut my hair severely short, expected to be treated badly by boyfriends and was. My emotional life became chaotic as I knew myself less and less and could no longer distinguish between what was important to me and what wasn't.

I seemed to have men coming out of my ears, but I was so restless that each one would become an alibi – anything to keep me away from myself. One diary entry from the time gives the flavour of it. On a certain Thursday evening I went to a gallery opening with one man, who'd dumped me a few months ago, and talked to him in an Irish bar about my current boyfriend. After getting home another ex and his friend called and said 'Come out for a drive', so I did. We went across the George Washington Bridge and over into Newark to look for wrestlers in a Howard Johnson's. No wonder I was confused.

Earlier on the night that I'd been mugged, Joseph had talked about his great poetic hero, W. H. Auden, as a man who had the courage to 'choose himself'. Auden himself had written, sanely:

> Crying for the moon is
> Naughtiness and envy,
> We can only love what-
> ever we possess.

from 'Heavy Date', *W. H. Auden: Collected Poems*,
ed Edward Mendelson (Faber and Faber, 1976), p. 207

I was hellbent on getting rid of myself. I was also trying to do this in the name of poetry, as if it were possible to substitute some poems for a life. Of course, this isn't how the creative mechanism works, and I had gone downhill so far that I was using poetry only to torture myself – the opposite of what it really is, a shot of reality, a comfort in trouble, an extra eye.

But the writing wasn't going well. No matter how I tried the poems sounded contrived, mannered, not like me – hardly surprising, given that I was so unhappy. One evening, I found a first edition of Dylan Thomas's *In Country Sleep* on the street, with the delightful 'Poem on His Birthday'. It seemed a good omen and reminded me of home. My apartment was so dark that, once spring came, I'd go out into Central Park to work. In desperation, I launched on a long poem describing my life in Manhattan, full of details of Hispanic families with their ghetto blasters in Central Park, phones ringing unanswered, like birds. You can't will poems to be good, and this one, though full of vivid details, was mawkish and full of self-pity. This, though, was its main virtue. It was long and honest enough to show me what

I'd become – a desperate observer of other people with no substantial life of my own. I didn't like it but this was the poem I needed to write before I could go home. It had caused me huge suffering, but at last I knew I was on the right track, could use form to bring me to truths about myself, and that I could carry on.

'God, you look ill', were my sister's first words when I met her at the airport. She had come to visit and was shocked at how thin and gaunt I looked and talked to me sternly about getting a job and a better way of life. Most of all, her company reminded me that this wasn't how I used to be, so that I could see, for the first time, the catastrophic decline in my own morale. Even my clothes had become dowdy. 'Gwyn, you know, the garret is over-rated', Joseph had said with a maternal look one time we met.

I finally reached a decision in April 1985. As usual, I'd been working on a bench in Central Park and, as he passed, a little boy whom I had often seen asked me 'Still sitting here?' It felt as though I'd been sitting there with the bums for years, was in danger of becoming a bum myself.

It was time to go home and make some kind of life.

CHAPTER SIX

CHAPTER SIX

A Resurrection

My resurrection started the day I managed to wear earrings again.

They say that Lazarus never laughed again after being brought back to life. His family was overjoyed, but did he remember them? Was he the same person?

Being dead changes you. Amnesiacs who've spent time in a coma never catch up on the life they've lost, become strangers in their own families. Some have altered so much that they can no longer love their spouses. Some then marry their ex-wives' supportive best friend whom they never noticed before the accident.

I had been kidnapped by depression and killed. The up side of being dead is this: without your usual energy you're really able to see what you are, how you've been living.

People who are depressed have stopped lying to themselves.

*

I took the lamp and, leaving the zone of everyday occupations and relationships where everything is clear, I went down into my inmost self, to the deep abyss whence I feel dimly that my power emanates. But as I moved further and further away from my conventional certainties by which social life is super-ficially illuminated, I became aware that I was losing contact with myself. At each step of the descent, a new person was disclosed within me of whose name I was no longer sure and who no longer obeyed me. And when I had to stop my exploration because the path faded from beneath my steps, I found a bottomless abyss at my feet, and out of it – arising I knew not from where – the current which I dare call *my* life . . . In the last resort the profound, like the new-born life, escapes our grasp entirely.

> Teilhard de Chardin,
> Quoted in *The Tao of Jesus*, ed Loya, Ho and Jih
> (Paulist Press, 1998), p. 125

Depression is a benevolent version of the woman being carried away in Goya's *Caprichos*. Something you've been doing in your life has taken your feet, for a moment, off the ground, leaving you vulnerable. Against your will, your desire and your better judgement, you're carried away from your own life. Except this time you're in skilful hands and will have to trust them.

Whatever returns to you after this abduction is your

real life. If you're wise, you'll wait for this life to come to you or risk the same old confusion between what was meant for you and what wasn't, your authentic life and your forgeries.

My resurrection was modest to begin with: I got up, put on clothes. I tackled supper, but it took me all day to cook a goulash that normally takes me an hour. I had to retire to bed for naps in between browning the meat, softening the onions and again before adding the paprika.

Willpower, the engine that used to drive all my activities, had deserted me. I had no idea when I got up every day whether or not I could stay awake, let alone do anything to which I might put my mind. Anything I did from now on had to be fuelled from a different source.

I had no idea what would happen next. All I could do was wait for it to happen.

> Don't look for beauty. You must let beauty come to
> you. Those who look for beauty are mere journalists.
>
> Borges

*

Depression happens to people who won't listen to the messages which their subconscious is sending them. Severe depression happens to those so wilful that they ignore whatever goes contrary to their conscious desires. If I had listened to myself sooner, I wouldn't have needed to get depressed.

Whatever your depression makes you do is how you should be living. It cuts out vast areas of interference caused by the forced life you've been conducting. Take special note of what it stops you doing. For me that was, in descending order, working too hard, torturing myself with the past and having no fun.

Being this ill gives a crash course in how to live. When I was young I remember seeing a film about Helen Keller, who was born blind, deaf and dumb, and her teacher who brought her out into the world. At the start, the deeply introverted child didn't want to leave her familiar isolation and learn sign language. But her teacher forced her, pressing the words into her palm like money she didn't know how to spend.

The process of drawing Helen Keller out was violent. This is what depression is doing to you. It's trying to teach you how to live in a world that's broader than you thought, but it's frightening. If you refuse to be teachable, depression can become even more forceful. If that fails then you're really in trouble, because your gods will finally have left you.

*

To believe in God is not a decision that we can make. All we can do is decide not to give our love to false gods.

Simone Weil, 'Three Essays on the Love of God', *Gateway to God*, ed David Raper (Collins, Glasgow, 1974), p. 75

There is a neurological condition where patients suddenly become convinced that a loved one has disappeared and their place has been taken by an impostor. No matter what proof they're offered, nothing can convince them that the look-alike is not a fraud.

The experience of coming out of serious depression is like this, except that the stranger in the house is you. Hell always leaves its mark on a person, even if all you did was eat a pomegranate seed while there. The person you were has gone forever. And that is the best news of all, though it might not feel like it at the time. I discovered new tastes, had unprecedented cravings. For example, I'd never made a bowl of porridge in my life, but I began to have it for breakfast every day knowing that I liked it not salted but with maple syrup and sultanas.

I developed a totally uncharacteristic passion for nail varnish and would tell anybody who rang 'Today I have Wild Lilac on my fingers and Black Tulip on my toes.' From being a person who would chew any varnish off my nails within half an hour of putting it on, I became captivated by Space Babe, Magical and Quartz. What's more, I changed my nail varnish colour every day until my nails became brittle from the acetate in the remover. I might have been Woman in a Dressing Gown, but my nails were manicured and polished.

The point of living in the dark of depression for so long is that you're being changed in ways that go beyond your conscious will. That has been knocked out for the duration for a good reason, like a dangerous power supply while your internal wiring is being repaired.

Anybody who tells you to do anything in this state is wrong. Let the process that's beyond you have its way with you. Or risk electrocuting yourself.

Widow in dark for twenty years over power cut

A pensioner lived in the dark for twenty years after her electricity supply was accidentally cut off and she was too embarrassed to tell anyone.

The woman, now a widow of 86, thought that she had been deliberately disconnected because she used so little power and her bills were too low.

She used candles and oil lamps from

1977 until one of her friends reported her plight to the Yorkshire Electricity Company.

A company spokesman said ... 'Because she had been without electricity for so long, her home needed rewiring before we could reconnect the supply.

'In view of her age, along with the fact that her husband has now passed away, we met the cost of providing a new supply and the rewiring of her home.'

Paul Stokes, *Daily Telegraph*

Even though it still looked like catastrophe, this stage of depression had a sensuality which took me completely by surprise. My first walk out was a pathetic affair by my usual brisk standards, but to me it was a triumph.

It was after dark and I crawled along the streets near our house, concentrating hard, as if I'd forgotten how to put one foot in front of the other. Leighton had to pause for me to catch up with him from time to time but because I was so slow I could hear the stream which runs alongside our local park. Its constant movement was soothing, so we stopped to listen. Then I noticed the pattern of rotting lilac shadows interspersed with willow branches on the pavement, and it had rhythm, looked like a William Morris design.

I wasn't able to go far on these walks but, when I could manage them, they were ravishing. In a burst of sunshine a rowan tree and its shadow became suddenly deeply three-dimensional against the corner of a house, making me stop. This is how children walk around streets which seem ordinary to us, seeing wonders everywhere.

Sleepwalker survives 60-foot fall

A British tourist was recovering in a Greek hospital last night after he climbed over the balcony of his fourth-floor apartment block in his sleep and fell 60 feet to the ground.

Roger Goodwin, 28, of Bloxwich, West Midlands, broke his fall by grasping the metal frame of a canvas awning and try-ing to swing, trapeze-style, into another flat.

His attempt, while still apparently asleep, failed but it was enough to slow his descent. Although he fell two more floors on to a concrete path, he was not seriously injured.

He said: 'I don't remember a thing – just the sight of people looking over me when I suddenly woke up.'

He added that he had suffered from two other sleep-walking experiences in the past two years 'but nothing like this.'
David Graves, *Daily Telegraph*

This is how depression guides you. You decide to paint your nails. That's fine, it lets you do it. You're feeling better, *Boiling*. You walk to the shop, buy a card for your sister. *Still Warm*.

Then you go too far. As well as writing the card you decide to answer all the letters that have piled up while you've been sleeping, including the tax.

Clunk. Morale collapses. *Freezing Cold, Getting Colder*. Defeated, you have to go back to bed upstairs. *Warmer, Warmer*. Put yourself to bed. *Scorching*.

You climb into a dodgem and it lets you drive for a while but the minute you're off the track, the power supply is cut and you're sitting there, going nowhere. Try again tomorrow.

*

I've always hated ironing. Until I met Leighton I would hang my clothes up and hope for the best. Having spent ten years in the merchant navy, he even irons his underpants, so when we started living together, I had to be housetrained.

Ironing's the perfect thing to do when you're depressed. It requires no creative input but it has easy victories, makes you feel that you're making good, orderly progress in your life without the expenditure of too much energy. It doesn't matter if it's done badly. The strange new me loved the smell of the weather on the clothes, the bread-like warmth of a pressed blouse. I noticed for the first time the sounds I made as I folded cotton sheets, the heavy breathing of a steam iron sighing over shirts, as if they were delinquent sons, the way silk sounds like an intake of breath . . . Once, I came to the end of a pile of clothes and asked, disappointed, 'What, no more ironing left?' When this happened, Leighton and I looked at each other in astonishment.

Life in the present was suddenly vivid. I started listening as I cut vegetables and enjoying the different degrees of crunch. I hadn't been aware of these sounds for a very long time. It was as if they could, at last, get through to my body. A layer of plastic between me and the world had dissolved. In the supermarket I walked past the freezer section twice, just to feel the cold pressing on me from both sides. I was back in the present, not living in the past, with its hall of mirrors.

I was coming back to my senses.

*

How noisy snowflakes drive fish to distraction

Snowflakes falling on water emit a piercing sound that may annoy aquatic animals and disrupt their sonar, a new study has revealed.

Researchers from four universities, including Edinburgh University, who analysed recordings made during winter storms, found snowflakes can add 30 decibels to underwater noise levels.

When snow lands on water it deposits a tiny amount of air just beneath the surface. Prof Andrea Prosperetti, of Johns Hopkins University, Baltimore, who is co-author of the study, told the Journal of the Acoustical Society of America: 'If you submerge a pocket of air trapped in a snowflake, that pocket of air cannot just sit there.

'The bubble has to adjust its volume and it will do so by oscillating. When it oscillates, it emits noise.'

The sound is too high-pitched for human ears but could affect porpoises and other aquatic animals that hear higher frequencies.

Snowflake noise can also create electronic 'clutter' for people using sonar to track migrating fish or to distinguish between natural and man-made underwater sounds.

> The research could help develop
> equipment to filter out sounds made by
> snow.
>
> Roger Highfield, Science Editor, *Daily Telegraph*

I've begun to see that many of my problems in the past haven't been due to having too little energy, but too much. This has led to overwork, doing things I shouldn't and generally becoming a liability to myself.

I've never really understood what the seven deadly sins were all about. I know you shouldn't commit them, but how do they work psychologically? Why are they bad for you? If you look at them as abuses of energy, they begin to make sense in a secular way. Sloth is the deliberate under-use of vitality, the refusal to act even when the necessary energy is available to you. It's refusing to take responsibility for your own basic emotional housekeeping. Gluttony is the intake of more fuel than necessary for the basic activities of life. Avarice is the same in the form of money accumulated for its own sake rather than as a means to an end. Pride, for example, is an over-investment in a misplaced and fixed view of your own importance, rather than a more fluid notion of identity that can place yourself on the periphery of the action.

Wrath, lust and envy are three forms of the misdirection

of energy towards objects which won't, in fact, help you to resolve anything. For example, envying the garden of a neighbour is a waste of energy because it's never translated into action. Much better to visit the garden centre and purchase a few pots of your own. All idolatry, of course, is the confusion of a means for an end in itself.

It's time for me to begin directing my energy more carefully. Except that depression, by pulling the plug on me from time to time, is already doing the choosing. All I have to do now is to follow my leader.

Sloth is really a busy condition, hyperactive. This activity drives off the wonderful rest or balance without which there can be no poetry or art or thought – none of the highest human functions. These slothful sinners are not able to acquiesce in their own being, as some philosophers say. They labor because rest terrifies them. The old philosophy distinguished between knowledge achieved by effort (*ratio*) and knowledge received (*intellectus*) by the listening soul that can hear the essence of things and comes to understand the marvelous. But this calls for unusual strength of soul. The more so since society claims more and more and more of your inner self and infects you with its restlessness. It trains you in distraction, colonizes consciousness as fast as consciousness advances. The true poise, that of con-

templation or imagination, sits right on the border
of sleep and dreaming.

Saul Bellow, *Humboldt's Gift* (Penguin, New York, 1975), p. 306

In my inner cosmology, if the ego's a noun, willpower is its
verb. Willpower is the ego's motor force. In a state of
depression, my willpower, along with my ego, had collapsed.

For example, I'd decide that I wanted to visit a friend.
Something inside me would object, telling me that I was still
far too weak, that I'd never make it, that even the attempt
would damage me. Physically, however, there was no reason
why I couldn't make the short drive to Canton. I coaxed and
threatened myself but to no avail. My willpower was like a
dog that had heard the bathwater running and had hidden
itself, refusing to come out, whatever the bribe.

I think that I abused my willpower for a long time before
I collapsed, forcing myself to do things that weren't right for
me, doing the right things for the wrong reasons or simply
doing too much. Over-activity's one futile way of persuading
yourself that you're still in control. For example, one of the
signs that I'm about to go down is a sudden mania for moving
furniture. The feeling is that if only I could manipulate the
set on which my life is lived perhaps I could avoid feeling
so shitty.

The problem with willpower is that it looks like a long-term source of energy but it's not. It's designed for short adrenalin-fuelled bursts, for steeling yourself for patently distasteful tasks like cleaning up vomit or doing the accounts. Now my willpower was having its revenge. As a gauge of what's good for me it's totally inaccurate and as a compass misleading. Willpower is a good servant, but a bad master; a powerful engine but a dangerous steering mechanism.

You can't will yourself better from depression, any more than you can will a good poem into existence. You'll get something, of course, but it won't have any lasting value because it will have been constructed from the top of the head rather than grown from the rhythms of the whole body.

One of depression's main messages is that you can't live as though you yourself are a renewable source of energy. Your exhaustion proves you're not. Real energy comes from outside yourself, so stop acting as if it didn't. Stop before you blow all your circuits!

> It's good to do nothing,
> and then to rest.
> Spanish proverb

*

What I needed was another form of transport, an alternative to willpower's combustion engine. I started to think of myself as apart from my own energy, like a rider and a horse. If a horse turned up on any given day, all well and good. If not, I'd walk. I learned to ride the energy horse I was given daily without carping about how slowly it went. The horse is non-negotiable. Of course, it's nice to feel the wind in your hair, but just accept the old nag you're given, even if she rests her chin on your head, sighs and keeps on stopping to graze on the verge.

Before I fell ill I was used to riding the kind of beast that gallops around doing things, ticking tasks off lists. A more leisurely pace, however, just gives you a different point of view and time to stop for a chat with Gerry and Sheila on the corner, you haven't seen them in ages.

It is said that there are four kinds of horses: excellent ones, good ones, poor ones, and bad ones . . .

If you think the aim of Zen practice is to train you to become one of the best horses, you will have a big problem. This is not the right understanding. If you practice Zen in the right way it does not matter whether you are the best horse or the worst one.

You will find that the worst horse is the most valuable one. In your very imperfections you will find the basis for your firm way-seeking mind . . .

Those who have great difficulties in practicing Zen will find more meaning in it. So I think that sometimes the best horse may be the worst horse, and the worst horse can be the best one.

Shunryu Suzuki, *Zen Mind, Beginner's Mind*,
ed. Trudy Dixon (Weatherhill, New York & Tokyo, 1998), pp. 38–9

I now found it impossible to tell how much energy I had at my disposal every day. Given that my energy-indicator had been broken I had to guess how much petrol was in the tank.

From my diary: 'Felt I couldn't cook in the evening, but decided to give it a go. Even tho' I felt terrible, managed a stuffed tenderloin of pork. Lesson: can operate through the fug, maybe I should try this, gently. Maybe the pills are what's making me so tired . . . Have no sense of what's real, or when I'm tired, so need to find another way of telling.'

Sometimes, of course, I judged it wrongly and had to abandon a shopping exhibition I'd started. Leighton and I learned to recognise this energy bankruptcy and when my 'arse' had 'hit the ground'. Once this had happened there was no argument. I went straight back to bed.

*

Depression is the modern TB, the disease of the sensitive. Can you imagine a sanatorium only for depressives? Depression isn't sociable, despite being common. You couldn't talk about the 'community of the depressed' because it's precisely the patient's ability to be with him- or herself and other people that's been eroded by the disease.

And yet, there is a certain similarity to TB, in the way that the temperament of the patient seems implicated in the disease. There was much talk in the past of the 'TB type'. Tell me, if I'm low, is that my melancholy character or a symptom of depression? In general, I'd say that I'm a cheerful, positive person, totally different from the stereotype of the melancholic. Throughout this whole episode of depression, I only cried twice. So much for the disease's stereotypes.

By now it was early spring and I was thoroughly sick of staying in bed, but I didn't yet have enough energy to be doing anything. One day I remembered that my gym had an outdoor swimming pool. It was a struggle, but I managed to get myself down there and changed into my bathing costume. I found a lounger away from the muzak piped throughout the building. It was so cold that I had to put on every scrap of clothing I'd brought with me and cover my legs with a towel. I lay there, like a TB patient of the 1940s, out in inclement conditions, trying to freeze my disease out before I caught my death of cold.

It wasn't glamorous but through half-closed eyes I watched the wind in the ground-cover bushes, the glint of occasional sun on the empty swimming pool. I couldn't swim, but I grabbed a float and played dead in the amniotic, wind-rippled water.

> A heavy snowfall disappears into the sea.
> What silence!
>
> Folk Zen Saying,
> Quoted in David Schiller, *The Little Zen Companion*
> (Workman Publishing, New York, 1994), p. 224

The difference between depression and despair is that despair is static, whereas depression, underneath its lassitude, is all about transformation. Depression is a temporary opting-out, to enable you to adjust to life more successfully. The process has its own dynamic, like water, and you can float on its surface if you trust its buoyancy.

Despair is much more dangerous because it insists on a fixed position. Even when adopted as part of an intellectual fashion, it doesn't allow for a way out of its own stance. It won't release you, as depression does, as a matter of course. No doubt it has its pleasures, but it's a mask that merges eventually with your face.

Where despair is a statue, depression is a waterfall.

*

For wisdom moves more easily than motion itself;
she is so pure she pervades and permeates all
things. . . . She is but one, yet can do all things;
herself unchanging, she makes all things new . . .

The Wisdom of Solomon, Chapter 7: 24–5, 27
The Apocrypha, *The Revised English Bible*

Then I started to get it.

Another sunbathing day. This one was more promising: a
white sky and the weather warm enough for me to lie still
in my bathers. I was struggling with myself, feeling miserable
for still being ill, trying to think myself out of my own
wretchedness. What was wrong with my attitude? Could I
think more positively and so make myself recover more
quickly? Should I take more exercise? What was it about my
past that had made this catastrophe happen?

Suddenly I decided to give it up as a bad job. All this
internal effort was getting me nowhere. I accepted fully that
I was feeling awful.

Immediately my mood improved. I started to observe my
day, rather than feeling responsible for it. A wiry old man
lowered himself gingerly into the pool, as if it were a particularly distasteful pair of trousers. He began to swim lengths,
slapping the water with his arms. I could hear the pop of

tennis balls being hit in the courts nearby, like corks shooting out of champagne bottles. The light flexed its muscles as clouds were moved on by the wind.

Paying attention to the world around you, rather than wishing to alter it, changes everything. Awareness allows the world to continue being itself without you raging at its refusal to conform to your will. It shows you the world as it moves, not in adjectives but in verbs.

At a stroke things had changed from freeze-frame to moving pictures. I began to enjoy the afternoon and the breeze on my skin.

At this critical moment it happened that a young officer who was sent to her [the daughter of King Christian IV of Denmark] misunderstood his orders and demanded that she take off all the jewellery she was wearing and hand it over to him. Although this ought to have startled her (since she was not yet aware that she was in any danger) and thrown her into the utmost alarm, nevertheless, after a moment's consideration, she takes off all her jewels – the earrings, the necklaces, the brooches, the brace- lets, the rings – and puts them into the officer's hands. The young man brings these treasures to his superior, who, at first terrified, then enraged, at this imprudence, which threatens to upset the whole undertaking, orders him, curtly and in the coarsest language, to return and give everything back to the Countess, and to beg her forgiveness, in any way he can think of, for this unauthorized blunder. What happened now is unforgettable. After considering a moment, not longer than that first moment was, Countess Ulfeldt gestures for the bewildered officer to follow her, walks over to the mirror, and there takes the magnificent necklaces and brooches and rings from his hands, as if from the hands of a servant, and puts them on, with the greatest attentiveness and serenity, one after another.

Tell me, dear friend, do you know any other story in which it is so sublimely evident how we ought to behave toward the vicissitudes of life?

Rilke, A Letter to Sidonie Nadherny von Borutin, Feb 4, 1912, Quoted in *The Selected Poetry of Rainer Maria Rilke*, ed and tr by Stephen Mitchell (Vintage, New York, 1984), pp. 307–8

The abyss of depression is a precious thing. It feels like sadness, like emotional death. But, just as winter isn't the absence of life, but only a stage in the cycle of vitality, feeling low is an essential part of living. Trying to avoid feeling this fallowness had nearly killed me. So why not lose my fear of dejection and learn to accept it?

Depression was teaching me to deal with lowness more positively. If you stop hating it, feeling down isn't half so bad. Not knowing where to go, after all, might be the most important part of travelling.

Julia Kristeva writes that her patients have to 'face the void' created by depression. The Zen meditations which I've learned offer a safe passage through meaninglessness, and prove that confronting it is part of being mentally stable. The Horrors soon pass if they know you don't intend to hold on to them.

> All sins are attempts to fill voids.
> Simone Weil, *Gravity and Grace*,
> (Routledge and Kegan Paul, London, 1952), p. 21

The day darkened and I found myself alone by the swimming pool.

Time passed and I felt a few spots of rain. By now I was lying on my stomach. I felt the individual drops on my skin, like pins and needles all over my back and legs. I thought about moving but couldn't rouse myself. Lying in the rain was lovely, as if my circulation, which had been cut off, had suddenly begun to flow again. Feeling was returning.

Who says that sitting in blazing light is the only way of sunbathing? Try the luxury of rain, I recommend it.

CHAPTER SEVEN

Identifying the Body

The partners and close family members of those who are depressed have a uniquely difficult task. They live in a volatile emotional climate and tread on shifting ground. How do you refrain from feeding the dark in which the depressed person lives, while still supporting that loved one? How can you be tolerant of an invalid without granting disorder complete licence? The most acute problem is this: how do you care for someone who's depressed without falling into despair yourself?

This chapter is for those who are struggling or have struggled with these dilemmas. This doesn't exclude depressives themselves. In this account of depression I'm the patient but, in the past, I've had to live around and sometimes in my mother's depression. Her illness and her way of dealing with it have coloured a central relationship in my life. So I write from a double perspective: as one who's seen the devastating experience of depression at the heart of a family's life, and now as a depressive myself, watching the effect of my disease on my husband.

Depression is a confusing, disorientating experience not only for the patient but also for anyone who comes close to it. The crucial thing is that the right person be identified as the invalid. In their efforts to avoid the pits of the living dead, depressives are sometimes very adept at placing blame for their distress on anybody except themselves.

I thought for years that I was directly responsible for my mother's depression. Make sure you and your family know who really is the corpse, because this kind of death can be catching.

1 Don't get depressed yourself

If there's anything worse than one person depressed in a family, it's two. However much you love them and whatever they're like when they're well, the clinically depressed are universal party-poopers. They have no energy, don't want to do anything. They see the down side of everything and, at best, are indifferent to the things that used to excite them. They don't want to get out of bed in the morning; they avoid washing, dressing, going out during the day, but they're wide-awake when you're ready to retire. In short, they become a nightmare teenager: anti-social, unreliable, self-centred, touchy and inconsiderate, brimming with a drama which seems entirely unnecessary to the rest of the world.

You begin to wonder why on earth you liked them in the first place.

One of the most heartbreaking things about depression is that, however much you love someone and whatever you're willing to do for them, you still can't save them. I know because I tried for decades. I thought that if I were a better daughter, my mother wouldn't fall into her pit of depression. This seems naïve now but it is still a deeply held belief of mine. It has made me do some very uncharacteristic things which didn't suit me, including writing a doctorate. I felt that if I dragged enough prizes back to our cave that she would be satisfied and not need to go through that hateful cycle again. In the end, my fantasy of rescuing my mother became a serious liability. It only ever did me harm and never did her any good.

The best you can do is to allow someone else to go through the experience in the easiest way possible. Feed them, by all means, field their telephone calls, but don't follow them. You have to allow other people their pain. If you don't, you risk losing everything for absolutely nothing because anything you can do from outside will never work. You could end up throwing your own life away and your relative or partner, at the end of it, will still be ill: a double defeat. At least, if you look after yourself, you have a chance of living your own life and are much more likely to be of help to your loved one.

I feel fierce about this because our family, when I was a child, allowed itself to be dictated to by my mother's depression. This had a disastrous effect on morale and on my sense of self. We could sense the onset of a storm and,

over time, we learned to recognise its build-up and to dread
its inevitability. I used to beg my mother not to do what she
was going to, but by then she was strapped into the emotional
rollercoaster and couldn't get off. For some reason I was
slower than my sister in anticipating what might prove
the flashpoint. Marian was adept at ducking when trouble
loomed. I, being more straightforward (or plain stupid)
didn't see the need to avoid confrontation, so it was usually
me who set off my mother's rage and her plunge into despair.
I was taught to try not to do anything that would enrage my
mother, a futile task because my whole existence seemed to
rile her sometimes. My father advised me to be more cunning,
less direct in saying what I wanted or meant and not to mind
when a simple request of mine brought the whole house to
a standstill for three days. But I did mind. He might as well
have been telling me that it was all my fault. The message I
received was that I'd blown it again and now we were all in
for it, so keep your head down, no matter how wretched you
felt. What he should have told me time and time again was
that it wasn't my fault and not to cry.

My father was doing his best in a difficult situation: a
lifetime is sometimes too short to learn how to deal with
this emotional enemy. What we were being taught by this
way of handling depression was that it was politic for the
rest of the family not to be too insistent in their emotions
because my mother's reaction might be too hot to handle.
My desires had to be subordinated to whether or not she
could cope with them or her own at any given time. This
felt inevitably like being upstaged. Knowing what I felt or

wanted was a liability because it could plunge us all into chaos and make the waiting for Mam to come round even more difficult to bear than it already was. Nobody talked to each other directly, Dad mediated between us all, pouring oil on troubled waters. The family was a unit: we had to come through my mother's moods together.

After the initial row and violent displays of frustration, Mam would crash out, retire to her bed for three days or so before gradually re-emerging to take meals with us and slip back into family life. During this time we tiptoed around the house, whispered behind closed doors and generally put our own lives on hold until Mam was back in the land of the living. We'd watch the television with the volume right down so as not to wake her. We'd jump if we heard her stirring upstairs or the bedroom door opening. We had no way of knowing what would happen next – whether we'd have to go through another round of bitter recriminations or whether we'd see her wandering round the house like a ghost. I don't know which was the more upsetting. I was always relieved when she went back to bed.

There is another way of doing it though. The depressed person should be allowed all the space in the world and a safe place in which to go through the worst of their suffering. But they shouldn't take over the whole house any more than an incandescent two-year-old should be allowed to dictate to the rest of the family. Children, especially, should be encouraged to carry on as usual, told not to feel guilty about their mother or father being ill and that, in fact, the best thing that they can do to help is to remain cheerful themselves. I can't stress this enough. If depression is not to do a family more damage than it already does, the other members must be given permission to be happy and to carry on with their own lives. They need to identify a cut-off point to enable themselves to maintain emotional autonomy. This doesn't mean being unsympathetic or harsh towards the patient but it does mean not giving your own life as a hostage to hell.

This is the difference between sympathy and empathy. I remember a lecturer in college trying to describe the difference between these two emotional attitudes. He sketched a scenario. You're on a riverbank and you see someone drowning in the water. If you feel empathy – the power of entering into the experience of another person – you might begin to hyperventilate on the bank, go into a state of corresponding panic and thus become totally incapacitated. If you feel sympathy, however, you're equally affected by the drowning person's affliction. Your feelings are in harmony with the difficulties being experienced but you would not literally reproduce them in yourself. Your compassion might, instead, take the form of running to fetch a lifebelt or even diving into the river and pulling them out. I know I'd take sympathy over empathy every time.

They say that a drowning man comes to the surface three times before he finally sinks. That is three chances to save him and yourself.

2 Don't let the depressive act it out

Depressives shouldn't be held to account for the way they feel but they should for the way they behave.

You can take it as read that any depressive has tried long and hard to alter the way he or she feels. They will have employed all the stratagems at their disposal to avoid entering the zombie zone. These might include overworking, getting drunk, getting laid, painting the house, taking a holiday, not taking a holiday, buying new clothes, taking them back or considering surgery. All these will have failed, so even if you move heaven and earth to make them feel better, and however much they love you, so will you.

No one has the right to tell another human being how they should feel. However, if that person is taking it out on you, being critical, vicious, blaming you for what isn't your fault, they should be called to account. The patient may not be responsible for their emotional condition, but they are responsible for their behaviour. They may feel wretched, angry and desperate but they've no right to make your life unbearable. It won't help them or you in the long run.

Leighton's become very adept at saying 'Oi!' to me and drawing this line in exactly the right place for us. If I'm unreasonably irritable or sniping at him without cause, he usually disappears. I now know to shut my mouth, take myself off into another room or to bed so that I'm not even tempted to have a go. Eventually that prickly wretchedness passes of its own accord, if you don't stoke it up into a full-scale fight.

Acting out is a waste of a good depression anyway because it produces a smokescreen and confuses you further about the causes of your discomfort. You've a much better chance of getting to the root of the problem and moving on into a new life if you refuse to lash out. Behaving like a monster might feel good for a moment, but its only result will be to make two people miserable rather than the original one.

Partners and relatives shouldn't be afraid of challenging the depressive on the grounds of acceptable behaviour. After all, the patient isn't mad, just ill. They should never be allowed to use the plea of diminished responsibility due to insanity. Even if there are denials and tears to begin with, in the end it's a relief to know the truth, and that can only improve how everybody feels.

I know my mother feels guilty for being depressed when we were younger. This seems totally nonsensical to me and a complete waste of time. A few apologies at the time when things got out of hand would have been much more useful, as markers between what was her excess and mine, between normal behaviour and depressive despair. Happily, over the years, my mother's depression has largely withdrawn. We now get on much better and have both become more experienced in the war with our mutual enemy.

3 Tell the truth and shame the devil

Because clinical depression is an extreme situation, soft-soaping the patient is insulting because he or she is fighting for their existential life. Frankness is far better.

At home we have a policy of 'no mercy', which means telling things as they are. If you don't do this, how is the poor depressive ever to feel that lifting of the spirits that happens when the truth of a situation is recognised? I remember one time I was feeling very insecure about something, scared that I wouldn't be up to the task. 'I'm inadequate!' I wailed to Leighton. 'Yes', he said calmly, 'you are.' This made me laugh out loud because, in one sense, it was true. The problem wasn't whether or not I was up to the job but my agonising about it. From then on I was fine. Another Leighton classic is this one, which he fired at me when I was busy being self-obsessed: 'There are two people in this relationship and you're not both of them.' Quite so.

4 Touch is comforting

When I was at my worst and couldn't even speak for misery, I found that there was immense comfort to be had from Leighton's hand on my shoulder. A simple touch made me feel less isolated and less like a ghost. Words are mostly useless but physical solidarity meant a lot.

5 Know when to push and when not

Most depressed people will already have been trying to goad themselves into action, to no avail, so the added pressure of someone else pushing will usually do no good at all. Far more comforting is a partner's permission to be ill for as long as you need. This is perhaps the most important help anybody can give a depressive. It doesn't sound like much but simple acceptance by a partner can speed recovery more than anything because time isn't wasted in feeling guilty about putting someone else through all this (and so forth, ad nauseam). I was extremely fortunate because Leighton willingly took over cooking and washing while I was at my most debilitated, so I was left alone to let the depression run its course. This is, obviously, far more difficult if you have young children to care for or other responsibilities which can't be put down.

However, sometimes a depressed person needs a little push to make him or her move, like a colicky horse being led round a stable or a drugged person being walked in the fresh air to stop them going to sleep because if they do they might never wake up again. It takes skill and experience to know when to pull the rope and when to let the patient be. Once I started to get better, Leighton was a complete bastard and insisted that I went to the supermarket with him. I remember one time crying all the way there in the car, complaining how tired and miserable I was but he kept insisting that I could do it and he was right. It took ages to gather what we needed, but I saw someone from work whose wife was going through something similar, so I felt much better for the chat and a sense of achievement for being out in the world.

There is an addictive element to being a withdrawn, depressed person and a real danger that you can become too fond of your cocoon. This needs to be guarded against, so a bit of spousal whip-cracking from time to time can encourage a reality-check and establish the parameters of what you can really do, as opposed to what you feel like doing which is, all too often, lots more of nothing.

6 Don't underestimate how tiring treading on eggshells can be

The person who looks after someone who's depressed really does have the shitty end of the stick because they have to live with the effects of a disease without undergoing the purgative experience of finally feeling better. We were very surprised that, as soon as I began to be well again, Leighton went to pieces. The load which he had been carrying for both of us suddenly became too much and he put it down because now, at last, it was safe for him to do so.

Paradoxically, the carer needing some care him or herself can help the patient as well. The Christmas before I finally went back to work, we decided that a holiday in Spain would do us the world of good. Everything was booked and we got ourselves up to a hotel in Heathrow the night before our flight. We had a leisurely meal and were just beginning to feel smug when disaster struck. Leighton began vomiting and spent the whole night with either his head or the other end over the toilet. The flight went without us and I drove us home, stopping off at every opportunity for more digestive evacuation. When we reached home, I congratulated

Leighton on not being sick in the car. 'I've had lots of practice keeping vomit down,' he said grimly, before heading for the bathroom.

He was so ill that Christmas that I had to take over. This improved my morale because I was pleased to be looking after him for a change.

It's hardly surprising that this illness should take a heavy toll on anybody who comes into contact with it. It requires the carer to keep faith with a person who's disappeared and left a corpse behind. More than patience is required. The carer should make sure they have someone outside the house to talk to when it all gets too much and it seems that their loved one is never going to come back. Get out, talk to people who are well to remind yourself what it is to be with the living.

Don't underestimate how tiring keeping cheerful can be. As a Western girl working as a hostess in a Japanese bar once commented, 'It is very ageing smiling all the time.'

CHAPTER EIGHT

The Alibi that Wouldn't Let Go

If you really want to be swept off your feet, forget men, try alcohol.

While in New York I had applied for a place to do post-graduate research at Oxford. I went up to Balliol in 1985 thinking that I would use my time in Oxford to write more poetry and work out my next move – back to the States, to London or home to Wales. I ended up writing a doctoral thesis on literary forgeries in the eighteenth century. I discovered that 'forgery' was a highly politicised term in the period, a way of labelling ideas as beyond the pale. Basically, if you liked an idea it was genuine, if you didn't it must be 'forged'. The irony of my preoccupation with authenticity didn't strike me at the time. My fascination with distinguishing between the genuine and the fabricated must, however, have been the echo of an internal struggle. What kind of poetry should come out of me? Was there a genuine Gwyneth? Which parts of me could be said to be fake?

I started conscientiously with my research. I didn't want

to be one of those ghostly postgraduates who never finished their theses and hung around Oxford with a traumatised look in their eyes well into middle age. I joined the poetry society and, after two terms, moved out of college lodgings down the Cowley Road, where I felt much more comfortable. I pushed myself to write and to send out poems to magazines. Slowly, I received some acceptances, the most important being a place in the *Poetry Review*'s New British Poets feature. Eventually I even won an Eric Gregory Award, given to young poets under the age of thirty, a vote of confidence in my promise, at least, and some crucial financial support.

But a shadow had followed me back from America. I was still prone to bouts of feeling down, even though everything appeared to be going extremely well. I had changed my life, moved to another continent and into a very different way of life and still I would go through periods of feeling utterly bereft. I began to despair of ever being free of these moods. Hadn't I already done everything I could to be shot of them? Nothing could touch my feeling of desolation during these downers. I began to use drink to blot them out.

Of course the drinking me didn't appear suddenly out of nowhere. My crisis with alcohol had a certain inevitability to it, looking at it retrospectively. Almost the first time I got really drunk, I lost my shoes, was sick in every toilet on the way home and had a blackout about what had happened at the party. My drinking had increased over the years but in step with my contemporaries so that I didn't stand out particularly. Gradually I'd earned a reputation as a 'good drinker' and had, on several occasions, sent men slithering under the table opposite me. After a heavy holiday in Scotland an acquaintance declared that he was only going to marry a Welsh woman because, after watching me all week, they must have amazing constitutions.

There is a big difference, though, between drinking heavily on social occasions and using alcohol to treat a mood that you can't shake. I remember being surprised at myself in New York after being mugged because I gave up drinking for a while. I knew that, struggling as I was with the after effects of the attack, I couldn't take the subtle self-distortions heavy drinking produces in an already depressed person. The outer assault had happened, and I needed to protect myself from its inner equivalent.

It's only a matter of time before any painkiller used too often loses its effectiveness and needs to be used in larger doses. Added to which, in Oxford, I fell in with a crowd of writers who were even heavier drinkers than I was, so my career as an alcoholic took a big step forward.

In alcohol I had found a chemical formula which made the self-abandonment which I had been practising spectacularly more efficient. Its action matched exactly my need for a reality away from my ordinary life. It allowed me to slip into a parallel universe at will. It was as if becoming drunk provided a wormhole into a universe with slightly less draconian rules of gravity, where I could move more easily. It was a place I preferred, certainly, to feeling depressed. It enabled me to shake that feeling of being 'all wrong' in the world, replacing that Gwyneth with a more sociable and fearless person. It was emotional cosmetic surgery whose effects never lasted into the following day, unless, of course, you carried on drinking.

In New York I had feared being carried away by some external force bent on my destruction. With alcohol, I thought I'd found a benign force with the same ability to transport and transform. Getting drunk was to re-enact internally the fate of Goya's *Capricho* woman. This rapture seemed less dangerous because I was administering it to myself and thought I had it in my control. In fact it was far more dangerous and was to cost me my sanity for a while.

Being a serious drinker involves a lot of falling over. Waking up after a particularly heavy session I'd find huge bruises all over my legs, as if I were still a child and hadn't quite mastered the co-ordination of eye and limbs. Shoes were a particular problem. Have you ever noticed how they seem to come off in traffic accidents or bombings? You see an injured person on the ground and there, near them on the pavement, laid neatly together are their shoes, as if the victim had just stepped out of them and into blood slippers. Shoes are just as eager to escape from drunks. Once I was coming down some stairs in new black high heels when one shoe went to the left, the other to the right, leaving me on my bottom in a tight skirt. The left shoe skittered timidly to the foot of the stairs while the right one zoomed away like a black cat and streaked up the staircase opposite. I managed to pick myself up but not without being seen by a party of smokers outside the common room. My shoes were duly returned to me and I was offered a cigarette.

Self-medication with alcohol also does strange things to your stomach. The summer my drinking really took off in Oxford it seemed to me that the standards of kitchen hygiene in all the take-aways down the Cowley Road had declined catastrophically. I told other people that I must be very sensitive to food poisoning because no matter what I ate with my drink, it seemed to make me vomit. My cure for such 'food poisoning' was usually three days in bed and packets of chicken noodle soup, with slices of fresh ginger cut into the brew for my 'delicate stomach'. I was sick a lot that summer as my drinking during the day increased. I'd surprise myself with my new capacity for spirits and was perversely proud of each new quarter bottle I could down on top of the rest. Then the next day I'd get the amount wrong or my body would rebel and I'd have to run to the toilet. I felt like a Roman in a vomitarium.

I've always been an 'all or nothing' person and, as with any other course of action, I applied myself conscientiously to my new alliance with drink. It was going to save me from my old enemy, depression. I discovered the delights of flat half-bottles of spirits, which you could slip into your handbag and take with you wherever you went: on a difficult bus journey, for example or, best of all, to the cinema where whisky and chocolate went down together beautifully in the back row.

Someone to whom I'd rashly confessed that I was drinking too much suggested that I abandon spirits and become a wine snob. Full of good resolutions, I took myself off to Oddbins for some research. The wine they had on offer that week was Cahors, a 'black wine'. I liked the sound of that and learned that it was made from quickly crushed grapes, that the must was boiled to produce a very tannic solution. The sign informed me that Cahors was the up-and-coming star in Paris. I went out with my purchase, feeling very continental. To this day that is the sum total of my specialist knowledge about wine. Frozen vodka suited me much better because it took you much further towards oblivion quickly and looked, at least, as innocent as water.

The number of poets who are heavy drinkers might tempt you to see being alcoholic as part of the artistic job description. Dylan Thomas has a good deal to answer for in this respect, even though the drink may not, strictly speaking, have killed him. Not only did he have curls, a Boat House and an Interesting Life, his poems sound like a lucid transcription of a drunken rapture. This, I can assure you, is very difficult to achieve and certainly can't be done while you're actually drinking. It's far easier to act like a poet than to be one. Writing good poetry requires acute self-awareness (as opposed to self-consciousness), a disenchanted eye, mental and verbal agility and considerable stamina.

It's easy to mistake the excitement of being drunk, when the walls are hissing at you and the loosened stays of your mind make strange new ideas pop into your head, with poetic inspiration. I know because I used to keep notes of my altered states of mind under the influence of drink, in the hope that the record of such trances would offer me new insights into my problems, or startling new images for poems. They didn't. If I could understand my handwriting afterwards, it was difficult to make any sense of what the words meant together. I was particularly fixated on the image of the old Severn Bridge as a guillotine; it seemed to come up every time I was drunk, as though I'd never thought of it before. I've never yet been able to use it in a poem.

I felt that I was increasingly being split in two, depending on whether or not I was drinking. Sober, I was still sensible, and beginning to realise that my new way of using alcohol might be becoming a problem. Drunk, however, I lost touch with what I knew I should be doing in order to lead the life I wanted. When I was drunk nothing that happened to me was my fault. I was the innocent friend who was put upon by other people. Life wasn't doing what it should by me – I deserved better. None of this was true, of course, and a drunk playing the Tragic Queen is a repulsive spectacle. As my health and behaviour deteriorated, I alienated some good friends, who I'm sorry to have lost.

My notebooks for that time show very clearly how the situation was getting worse. From writing a diary entry every day, my note-keeping had become fitful. The number of books which I read and from which I took notes had declined steeply because I could no longer concentrate long enough to finish anything. The diaries were full of euphemisms, such as: 'Another Bad Day'. This meant I'd done nothing but drink too much and suffer from the heebie-jeebies. On such days I would even look forward to the Australian soap, *Prisoner Cell Block H*, which can only be called acceptable entertainment if you're out of your skull.

I was sleeping badly and having nightmares. Soon my transcriptions of these epic struggles were taking up more space in my diary than my daily life. In fact, this shadow world was becoming more real to me than anything else. Sober, I could look out of myself and see the world reasonably accurately. Drunk, however, my head became like a lit room at dusk with the curtains left open. No matter how I'd peer out, I could never see past my own reflections. I kept on catching my own guilty eye, while a more wholesome world went on its way beyond the distorted me in the glass.

Soon, even my dreams seemed to be warning me that things were going very wrong. Here's one:

> Dreamt I visited New York . . . I'd been on a ferry.
> I was coming down some very steep stairs on the
> quayside when I dropped a carrier bag with an
> Oxford English Dictionary and a bottle of champagne in it. Tried to find it. Bag had fallen on to a
> ship, which was lurching and bucking about alarmingly, so that I had to hold on fast not to be crushed
> between it and the quay. I found Hugh and Sue and
> they said they'd help me find my way to the place
> where I'd dropped the bag. I managed to salvage the
> bottle of champagne.

'You'd have done better to choose the *OED*', a friend commented dryly. I must already have been unconsciously aware that if I carried on like this, I could kiss being a writer goodbye.

I remember the day even writing turned on me. When I was a teenager and we'd moved to the new house in Penylan, my bedroom, which looked over the whole city, had a flat roof just below its windowsill. Although I loved the view, I was very afraid that a burglar would easily be able to climb up into my room at night. In a drunken conversation I remembered this detail and decided to try it out in a poem. The piece described a burglar coming into my room and raping me. The narrative voice was ambiguous towards the strange violent man – half longing for him, half in dread. What astonished me, though, was the rage against my father, whom the voice in the poem seemed to blame for being unable to protect me. This was all so overtly sexual and screwed-up that I went into shock. It sounded as though I was half in love with the figure who'd attacked me in New York. Far from being a woman who was being carried away against her will, here was a poem telling me of violence I was wishing on myself. I stopped writing completely because by now I was in such bad mental shape that I couldn't face what my own work was telling me about my state of mind. It was to be a very long time till I could risk the lie detector, poetry, again.

Without the discipline of writing acting as a brake on my daily life, things deteriorated even further. Now I found myself unable to resist the hair of the dog to alleviate typhoidal hangovers. If a drink was like a wormhole in time to a different state of cognition, I seemed to fall into the holes increasingly frequently and on less and less of a pretext. I had been using alcohol for some time to blot out events and thoughts I didn't like. By now, however, it was taking over on occasions when I desperately wanted to be present. After reluctantly taking a drink I'd be kidnapped into the parallel, pissed universe, where I could only be ineffective and confused.

For example, during one holiday I managed to persuade my mother to come up to see me in Oxford. She was to stay the night and I was really looking forward to the visit. On the afternoon she arrived we went round Blackwells and spent too much money on books. In the evening we went to our local Italian restaurant where Mam had garlic bread for the first time. Even though I wanted to talk, I drank so much of the House Red that I soon became incoherent. 'Your eyes are rolling' Mam observed in that family tone of voice. After she'd left the following day I was heartbroken. I'd absented myself on an occasion which was really important to me. The problem was I was rapidly losing the ability to choose. Whenever I took a drink – and I never refused one – I was incapable of controlling what happened.

In a rare moment of desperation coinciding with lucidity, I decided with a boyfriend that we were drinking too much and that we had to go on the wagon. By now I was writing up my thesis and had already been exercising what for me was heroic restraint, in order to produce a coherent first draft. I confined myself to two glasses of wine after a long day's work. This was so successful that, for a while, I managed to 'forget' my rackety record with drink. After a more toxic end-of-chapter celebration than usual, we made a pact and poured all the drink in the house away.

God, it was miserable with only the thesis for distraction. Evenings rolled endlessly out in front of us and, sober, the TV was boring. We'd go for long walks at night, just for something to do. One evening my friend happened to mention a video-watching party he'd once been to, where the company drank a bottle of whisky. This vision of warmth and companionship reduced me to tears of longing and self-pity.

Alcoholism dovetails disastrously well with depression because both are symptoms of a refusal to face reality. Alcohol is, of course, a depressant, and the amount I'd been drinking would have made a rhinoceros suicidal. I'd stay in bed for days unable to do anything but read Modesty Blaise cartoon books (which I recommend highly to anybody incapacitated in this way). What I didn't know then was that depression is part of the solution to the problems in your life and not the main difficulty itself. Whereas I might have been able to listen to what my inner sense of survival was telling me had I not been drinking myself silly, as it was I only became increasingly lost and confused about what was wrong. I became so lonely that I was afraid to sleep at night without the radio on. However much I tried to live as I knew I should, I couldn't do it. Weighed down by alcohol, I couldn't work up the escape velocity to pull away from the terrible gravity of my situation.

Drink had become my alibi from myself. It had started as an occasional respite but had become a false life from which I couldn't escape. If my depression was telling me that an internal crime against myself had been committed, with alcohol addiction in the picture I had no chance of knowing my whereabouts nor the nature of the crime. All I knew was that I could no longer go to sleep while there was a pain barrier still ahead of me. Evenings became a race between me and oblivion. Could I drink enough to get to sleep before my true situation hit me? If I judged it right I'd manage to crawl to bed and crash out. If, however, I miscalculated the amount of alcohol needed to stun me, the prospect was terrifying: being awake at 2 am with nobody to phone, no one to hear you scream as the rollercoaster headed vertically down.

On a visit to my doctor I managed to blurt out that I was in a terrible mess, couldn't get out of bed or do any work. I didn't mention alcohol but my doctor sent me to see one of the university's counsellors to see what might be the best way to proceed. The lady who saw me was very helpful. She told me that I had to stop presenting myself as a blank canvas to others. One problem was that I was allowing people to paint their fantasies on to me so that when I finally let them know what I was like or what I wanted, I was already in too deep for the extrication to be painless. After the first session I was so pleased with myself for beginning to face up to my problems that I went home, bought myself a bottle of champagne and discovered by accident the wonderful mood-altering properties of cold remedies mixed with alcohol.

Somehow I was offered a job with a television company

in Cardiff, for whom I'd done some research the year before. I'd done good work for them on a current affairs programme in France, mainly by making sure that I stayed off the pop for the duration of the contract. It was 1989 and perestroika and glasnost in the USSR were setting off nationalist revivals in the Baltic states. I was sent to Estonia to research two programmes. Estonian is one of those fiendishly difficult and idiosyncratic Finno-Ugric languages. However, I found that if you drink enough vodka, you can understand Estonian. I was in Tallinn for the White Nights, the midsummer period when it hardly gets dark at all. I'd become friendly with our interpreter and spent long nights partying with her and her friends. Early on midsummer morning, after I'd made my linguistic breakthrough into Estonian, I refused the bottle of Chivas Regal being passed around. Something inside me had given way. I couldn't find a taxi so I walked back to my hotel through the broad Soviet avenues, feeling nothing.

Something *had* broken chemically inside me because from then on my tolerance for alcohol disappeared. From being able to down tequila slammers all night and still operate in some fashion the following day, I now became smashed on a glass or two of wine.

I moved back to Cardiff to begin my job in May, and was able to see my true situation. Being back in my home town reminded me that I hadn't always felt so wretched and bewildered. On evenings after work I'd make sure I was holed up in my house by 7 pm because any later and I'd be too drunk to drive. I bought my first car and promptly crashed it. I didn't make any effort to re-establish contact with old friends.

My life was now little more than working, then getting drunk on my own in front of the TV.

One evening I knew that I was going mad. My emotions, always volatile in recent years, now went completely haywire and I could see that I was about to fall into depths of which I'd previously had no conception. I felt as though I was skating on ice – everything that had given me any stability before had disappeared. My head spun with a new mental vertigo, as things shifted with soul-sickening speed. This was a place from which I knew I couldn't return.

For a split second I knew what it was to be beyond human help.

Just as quickly, I knew that I wanted to come back out of the shadows and into the sun.

CHAPTER NINE

Learning to Fall

The test of how successful your depression has been in transforming you comes when you begin to live again.

After a summer of sunbathing – lying like a medieval queen on my sunbed sarcophagus – and floating in the swimming pool, I began to be able to do things on my own initiative. Instead of being passive, I was able to exercise my willpower to a certain degree before it collapsed again.

For a number of years we'd spent summer weekends down on the Gower peninsula, beyond Swansea. Leighton's parents had taken him on holiday there just after the war, in chalets built to house Swansea residents escaping the blitz. The weather was so cold that they had slept wrapped in newspapers, waking themselves up with the crinkling. They had a wonderful time so, one Sunday, he and I went to see if we could find these cabins in the wooded cliffs behind the beach. To our surprise they were still there, higgledy-piggledy hill-billy chalets – named 'Balmoral' and 'Cowpat' – dedicated to the simple pleasures of eating, resting and wearing as few clothes as possible in the sea air.

We ended up buying a 1940s day hut called 'The Retreat'. The previous owner had worked in the steel industry, so the original wooden hut had been patched up with tin sheets and the whole construction cobbled together with six-inch nails. It had no electricity, no phone and had only recently acquired running water. I loved it.

We had missed the whole summer there because I'd been too ill to leave home. Now, however, I was starting to sit up and look about me, so I took myself off down to the cabin and ended up spending most of October there on my own.

It was then that I began to feel life moving under me again. Life began to possess an element of flow to it, rather than being as jerky as a drill bit stuck in a resistant wall. I had to learn how to ride this energy now in a different way: how to fall off, this time without hurting myself.

> Everything changes and moves to and fro, and that
> movement is God. Leo Tolstoy,
> Quoted in 'Introduction', *War and Peace*,
> tr Rosemary Edmonds (Penguin, 1957), Vol I.

*

I knew that I had to get myself moving, so I'd go out walking as often as I could. I'd go expecting nothing. I'd move my limbs and the world changed around me. The first walks were simply a matter of moving in time, just being aware of my surroundings again. All I had to do was observe and respond to the landscape. By now I was noticing just enough of my environment to prevent me from thinking about how I was.

One day I walked along the sedate cliff path from Caswell to Langland, a bay with bathing huts and benches along the beach. I was so tired by the time I reached there that I thought I'd have to catch a taxi back to the shack.

Instead, I sat on the sea wall and people-watched, seeing the light flexing its muscles, feeling the wind and, despite myself, changing my point of view. I observed as walkers ambled to the verge of the sea, greeted the edge, stood there, as if facing their greatest fear. The walkers were key witnesses in the afternoon's case against itself, and their pictures were taken by the flashing breakers.

Down on the beach two dogs were figure-skating in the sand, creating perfect figures of eight as they chased each other around their owners.

*

Girl marries dog

An Indian girl aged four has married a stray dog in a traditional Hindu service.

The ceremony was prompted by an astrologer who told the girl's father that the ceremony would transfer the evil effects of the planet Saturn from the girl to the dog, named Bullet.

The girl, Anju, had suffered several illnesses and had fallen into ponds, fractured bones and burnt her hand in the kitchen, said her father Subal Karmakar.

Anju was married in front of 150 of the 250 residents in a village, a cluster of fifteen huts amid paddy fields thirty-five miles north of Calcutta. Villagers said they enjoyed the sight of the girl garlanding the dog. They then helped the dog to put a garland around the bride with its paws.

But although residents enjoyed the feast, they ridiculed the ceremony. 'He is superstitious, but why should I care if he wants to waste money and give us a feast?' said one.

Anju's father was unrepentant. 'I did the right thing. My grandfather arranged a marriage of a relative with a dog forty years ago and the remedy worked,' he said.
Reuters

*

Someone once told me a story about a couple who went to climb a mountain in North Wales. Their elderly labrador refused to be left behind and followed them all the way up to the peak. By this time the arthritic dog was in a terrible state, completely unable to go another step.

The dog was far too heavy to carry. Its owners thought about calling Mountain Rescue but decided that you couldn't call out a helicopter for a dog. By then it was already late afternoon. While the woman stayed with their pet on the summit, the husband ran home in the lengthening shadows and returned with food, water and blankets.

They both spent the night on the mountain with the dog. In the morning, it had revived sufficiently to make its way slowly down the valley with its owners. I don't know what moves me more about this story: the determination of the ageing dog, despite its decrepitude, to be with its owners, or the compassion they showed towards their foolish pet.

I think I've worked out the whole dog thing. People admit into their lives a creature which is slower than their own thinking, which can only do them good. The animal requires basic care – regular outings each day, food, comfort – everything that people find so hard to give themselves. So, by stealth, owning a dog gives people a healthy life which their conscious selves would otherwise veto. Using the pretext of a pet, the owners slow down, get out and make a commitment to living at their body's pace without appearing to be selfish.

This British love of pets is, therefore, highly misleading. It's a spiritual matter in heavy disguise. What people in the park are really doing, as they throw a ball for Tyson or Slipper, is taking their own souls for a run.

I've never understood why depression is called 'the black dog', as if it were something outside yourself. This isn't to belittle the fear of dogs: I remember how, as a child, dogs' muzzles were about level with your throat, their every movement unpredictable. Nietzsche's description of a person having 'fierce dogs in the cellar' (*op cit*, p. 64) makes more sense to me than Churchill's labrador. After all, it's only by facing your fear of those trapped dogs that you can reach the treasure locked in the cellar with them: your real life.

Oh what is the barrier that stands out against this happiness, and what are the wolfish words upon our lips that deny it, the words that are not our words? What is the dog within us that howls against it, the dog that tears and howls, that is no creature of ours, that lies within, kennelled and howling, that is an alien animal, an enemy? It is the desire to tear out this animal, to have our heart free of him, to have our heart for ourselves and for the innocent happiness,

that makes us cry out against life, and cry for death.
For this animal is kennelled close within, and tearing out this animal we tear out also the life with it.

Stevie Smith, *The Holiday*, (Virago, 1986), p. 62

The best thing about being down the shack on my own was
not having to answer Leighton's anxious 'How are you?' every
day. If I felt rotten, there was no need to feel guilty because
I was making his life a misery, as well as my own.

In the best way possible, living in my hut allowed me to
'lose the plot'. Although I made sure I was looking after
myself – I ate well, slept whenever I needed to, read novels
with gusto – I was being taught that the meaning of every
day was none of my business. Indeed, part of depression's
work had been to hit, with its heavy stick, my fingers off
evaluation altogether. Judging whether or not I was doing
well had become irrelevant to living – all I had to do was
turn up. The only question to ask was 'is what I'm feeling
real or fake?'

There are enormous pleasures in acknowledging you don't
know what the hell is going on. Indeed, in San Francisco,
tourists are so enchanted by the city's daily fog that they take
the tour boat out into the Bay to listen to the narrational
tape for sights that they can't even see.

*

There is a Chinese story of an old farmer who had an old horse for tilling his fields. One day the horse escaped into the hills and when all the farmer's neighbors sympathized with the old man over his bad luck, the farmer replied, 'Bad luck? Good luck? Who knows?' A week later, the horse returned with a herd of wild horses from the hills and this time the neighbors congratulated the farmer on his good luck. His reply was, 'Good luck? Bad luck? Who knows?' Then, when the farmer's son was attempting to tame one of the wild horses, he fell off its back and broke his leg. Everyone thought this very bad luck. Not the farmer, whose only reaction was, 'Bad luck? Good luck? Who knows?' Some weeks later the army marched into the village and conscripted every able-bodied youth they found there. When they saw the farmer's son with his broken leg they let him off. Now was that good luck? Bad luck? Who knows? Anthony de Mello, *Sadhana: A Way to God*, (Image Books, Doubleday, New York, 1984), p. 140

I began to see that my perfectionism had hidden extreme wilfulness. Self-recrimination on the scale I've been practising it is a secret form of arrogance, because it assumed that if only I'd got things right (instead of wrong) I would have had control over their outcome. This was still relying on the ego as the primary source of energy, the self as the main reference point in life. Extended back into the past, this dwelling on my own fault had become an intolerably heavy burden to carry, a terrible instrument of self-torture.

And yet, I'd do almost anything to keep carrying this burden, because the alternative is too frightening: that I have no control over my own life. Ironically, the days on which I give up this grasp over my own business are my happiest and healthiest.

In *Beowulf*, the hero never reproaches himself when things go wrong, he just accepts it and says, 'God allowed it.' The hero is totally committed to action but not to the outcome, which is up to God.

> Little Kay was quite blue with cold – nearly black, in fact – but he did not notice it, for she [the Snow Queen] had kissed his shiverings away, and his heart was nothing but a lump of ice. He spent his time dragging sharp, flat pieces of ice about, arranging them in all sorts of ways, trying to make something out of them – it was rather like the kind of thing we sometimes do with small flat pieces of wood when we try to make patterns from them – a Chinese puzzle they call it. Kay made patterns in the same way, most elaborate ones, a sort of intellectual ice-puzzle. In his own eyes the patterns were quite remarkable and of the utmost importance – that was what the grain of glass that was stuck in his eye did for him! He would lay out his patterns to form

written words, but he could never hit upon the way
to lay out the word he wanted, the word 'eternity'.
The Snow Queen had said, 'If you can work out that
pattern for me, you shall be your own master, and
I will present you with the whole world – and a new
pair of skates.' But he could not do it.

Hans Christian Andersen's Fairy Tales, tr L. W. Kingsland
(Oxford University Press, 1984), 'The Snow Queen', pp. 267–68

Before I was able to concentrate enough to read again I
suddenly felt like doing a jigsaw puzzle.

My mother brought me a street map of Paris, one of my
childhood favourites. My technique has always been to sort
the pieces into groups with similar colours or shapes. In
Paris's case I had green for parks; avenues and roads in white;
the Seine in blue; assorted buildings and a large patch of
pieces with writing on them. When Leighton said, looking
over my shoulder 'Why don't you sort them out by shape?'
I warned him, 'Touch my jigsaw and you're dead.'

I found putting a world together again profoundly therapeutic. This is what Paris taught me: that the idiosyncratic
is the easiest to piece together. After I'd assembled the one-off
ideograms – the Eiffel Tower, the Toulouse Lautrec poster
that stood for Montmartre – the writing was the next easiest.
But, as the puzzle went on, I was left with all the pieces
which were difficult to distinguish from each other and then,

finally, a series of roads with *Ave de*, *Rue de*, *Bld de* and then only *de*. These final, crucial distinctions were the most difficult to make but also the most gratifying. Two pieces might look totally alike but describe places on opposite sides of Paris.

The easiest things to see aren't the most important in a puzzle. It's the pieces that look like background which require the most subtle discriminations. Guilt is easily mistaken for love.

Danger claim against dog lacks teeth

A housewife accused of keeping a dangerous dog was acquitted yesterday after a court was told that her pet lacked teeth.

Maxine Turner, 30, was charged under the Dangerous Dogs Act after two elderly women complained that her dog, Beth, growled menacingly as they passed her home in Aberporth, Cardiganshire.

Beth, a thirteen-year-old mongrel, faced being destroyed if Miss Turner was found guilty.

Colin Taylor, defending, told Cardigan magistrates that the Act could not apply to a canine without canines.

Mrs Turner said: 'All her teeth dropped out two years ago. She can't even
chew her dog food.

'What is she going to do – lick people
to death?'

Neil Tweedie, *Daily Telegraph*, 6 April, 2001

Destroying Paris was even more fun than constructing it.
Any such fixed picture is only a point of view at a certain
time, and can't be permanent. Once you accept this, its
destruction is hugely comforting because it conforms not to
what the ego would like – which is permanence, unchange-
ability – but to the shifting nature of reality itself.

If this depression had taught me anything it was not to
resist this breaking up and flow. It will happen anyway,
whether you want it or not. What I didn't know before was
that consenting to it brings great joy.

After Paris, I tackled the world.

A widower who was sent a jigsaw as a
birthday present was stunned when he
had completed the 1,000-piece puzzle to

discover that his late wife featured in the holiday scene.

Stuart Spencer, 62, said yesterday that he 'could not believe my eyes' when he spotted that one of the figures in the jigsaw of the Norfolk Broads scene – sent to him as a present by his daughter Trudi, 29 – was his wife Anne, who died in June 1997.

'It was an amazing coincidence to see her,' said Mr Spencer, of Ludham, Norfolk. 'The chances of discovering your late wife in a jigsaw must be higher [sic] than winning the lottery.

'It was impossible to recognise her from the picture on the front of the box because she was so small. But once I made the puzzle you could see her.

'First I saw her wheelchair, then I recognised her striped black and white T-shirt. It was a pleasant surprise and has brought back happy memories.'

The jigsaw showed Mrs Spencer, who died from diabetes complications, in her wheelchair on the back of the paddle steamer *Southern Comfort* on the Broads . . .

Mr Spencer said: 'I feel she has been immortalised in this puzzle. It is a wonderful keepsake.'

David Sapsted, *Daily Telegraph*, 20 January, 2001

*

It must be true that we are *savants* without knowing it. How, otherwise, can you explain the odd moment in assembling a jigsaw when, without thinking, your hand goes unerringly to the right gap with the correct piece? You suddenly know that a fragment which you've tried time and time again is right, and you're totally confident in its smooth click into place, even before the conscious brain has decided that it's found the solution.

These moments of inspiration suggest that what Zen tells us is true – we instinctively know what's right, but that we've forgotten it. The *koans*, or riddles, used by Zen masters to flummox their students and to short-circuit the rational part of the brain (the most famous being: 'What is the sound of one hand?') are like jigsaw puzzles. Reality's cut up into pieces we don't recognise. After you've struggled enough with discursive thinking, the process seizes up completely. It's then that the intuitive answer rushes in. The hand, almost without looking, picks up an unrecognisable shape and completes a continent.

Depression is also a jigsaw puzzle, or a *koan*, because it stops all your habitual ways of thinking and gives you a chance to listen to your own inspiration about your life.

As I recovered I realised suddenly that what I believed about my life wasn't true – that the opposite was the case. Far from being a curse, my desire to write was a blessing. My only crime had been to doubt it. I couldn't blame other people for anything. All my worries about the effect of my writing on other people were just a form of my own doubt, a projection of my own uncertainty and laziness.

Whereas I'd been abandoning myself to look for what I wanted outside, everything I longed for was already there, if I could keep faith with it. Far from being a victim of other people, I'd been doing nothing but bullying myself.

'This intimation of grace would sometimes last for several minutes, which made Bartlebooth feel as if he had second sight: he could perceive everything, understand everything … He would juxtapose the pieces at full speed, without error, espying, beneath all the details and subterfuges intended to obscure them, this minute claw or that imperceptible red thread or a black-edged notch, which all ought to have indicated the solution from the start, had he but had eyes to see: in a few instants, borne along by such exalted and heady self-assurance, a situation that hadn't shifted for hours or days, a situation that he could no longer even imagine untying, would be altered beyond recognition: whole areas would join up, sky and sea would recover their correct locations, tree trunks would turn back into branches, vague birds back into the shadows of seaweed.'

Georges Perec, Life A User's Manual, tr David Bellos
(The Harvill Press, London, 1987), pp. 338–39

*

I stayed up late to complete the world. The continents came together quickly at the end because the more jigsaw pieces there were in place, the fewer positions were possible for the remaining cups and ears. The closer you get to the end of the puzzle – all the main structures are in place and you're only filling in details now – a necessity of numbers takes over and you feel that you're not doing anything, that the picture's assembling itself.

In Toys R Us they had allegedly the most difficult jigsaw in the world: a dish of baked beans, with no plate showing through. I bought it for Mam. My third jigsaw was *Wild Poppies* by Monet, my most ambitious yet. Impressionists don't do outlines, so making progress with the puzzle was a matter of matching subtle gradations of colour. You wouldn't believe how many different shades of vivid red there are in a field of poppies. And the clouds were murder.

After working hard on these jigsaws, I began to see the world in patches: a papier-mâché sky with different layers of cloud moving at varying speeds, doing its Dance of the Seven Veils. Leaves growing along the planes of the sun's slant at certain times of the day. Blue tits showing themselves in splodges of uniform, just enough to let us know they're there. And spider threads attempting to sew these fragments together.

The basic unit of life is the intake of breath. Each in-breath is a piece of mosaic which, on its own, means very little but which, taken all together, adds up to a story. The person who breathes, though, isn't the one who forms the overall picture. Her job is to finger every exquisite block in gold, lapis lazuli or even plain terracotta and to forget how they might eventually go together.

These rules allow you to put the past down. Whatever you've done, cause and effect is rot and won't help you to slot today into place. What you thought was the overall plot is only stopping you now from assembling the real picture. Today's puzzle isn't about you, or the past. It's a beach on the Gower, and that white piece there is a wave.

Depressions, which are low-pressure systems, are the principal sources of cloud, poor visibility, rain and strong winds outside the tropics. They are highly mobile systems several hundred to a few thousand kilometres in diameter and their general direction of movement is eastwards, although they may move in any direction. Anticyclones are high-pressure systems and are characteristically areas of light winds, good settled weather. They are rather slow-moving and as a rule considerably more extensive than depressions.

The Times Atlas and Encyclopaedia of the Sea,
ed Alastair Couper (Times Books, 1989), p. 47

*

I'd always thought that 'low pressure' referred to the low numbers registered on a barometer. Meteorological depressions are very different, though. High pressure pushes an atmosphere down and creates stable weather conditions. Air under low pressure doesn't fall, it rises and so is unstable. Weather conditions in a depression are, therefore, volatile and draw in moisture-carrying winds from the sea. The void at the centre of the weather system is what brings in the rain. The rain is an accident of the depression and not its cause.

I think I might have got the relationship between my moods and the reasons for them totally wrong.

Until now whenever I felt low, my impulse was to look for psychological reasons to explain it – as if I needed a narrative to go along with every disordered mood. All the difficulties I'd had in the past (I could take my pick: there were plenty of stories) would supply a rationale for my present suffering.

But what if it's not like that at all? What if the way it works is that I feel low and that creates an emotional vacuum in me. That low pressure sucks in all kinds of old stories which 'fit' that mood. I grab hold of those stories, chew on them endlessly, because they fill that terrible void. In reality there's no necessary relationship between these stories and the depressed mood that drew them in. They're there by accident.

Could it be that for every pitch of mood, of sadness, for example, I've devised a precise story (one based, perhaps, on how I felt when that event happened)? And that narrative is now my label for that particular mood timbre, so that I call it 'I hurt X' or 'I let Mam down' or 'I haven't got children'?

This would be fine if I read this just as a label, like the Latin name of a plant. But always, always, I take this as an invitation – no, as a command – to replay the old stories yet again, to try, finally, to work them out in myself. It's no surprise that I fail every time.

> Tropical depressions moved in and out like trains, pulling their high precipitation, Force 8 winds and immoderate sea states behind them, and they always got a big welcome from me. The inevitable thunder and lightning overtures were exhilarating but I had been taught to observe them analytically, counting off the seconds between flash and boom at the rate of five to the mile, tracking the approaching storm, anticipating the foaming onset of the rain itself – comforting, cooling, charging the house with smells from the dripping garden; perhaps it was atmospheric electricity that sent mysterious squalls of frangipani and jasmine gusting through the rooms and lingering in fragrant air pockets long after the rain had gone. I liked the sense of privacy it invoked, the way towering curtains closed around the island and sealed it off from the rest of the world.
>
> Alexander Frater, *Chasing the Monsoon* (Penguin, 1997), p. 2

*

If I'm right about this, it changes everything about my inner weather system.

It means that I can ignore the invitations to self-recrimination that these stories offer, because they're not real, but random emotional meteorological events. They're not tasks sent to me by a wiser self, but red herrings. Trying to solve them has been a total waste of time because they're not real, they're just passing clouds, accidents of my local atmospheric pressure system.

They might be clues that I'm about to start feeling low, but they're not supernatural hints, not the fate to which I'm doomed. It's only through my following their each and every prompting to reproach myself that I myself have made them so. Ever since the original events happened it's me who's been the torturer-in-chief.

If I hadn't found this out, I'd have wasted my life.

Again and again I request you to be merry, if anything trouble your hearts, or vex your souls, neglect and condemn it, let it pass. And this I enjoin you, not as a divine alone, but as a physician; for without this mirth, which is the life and quintessence of physic, medicines, and whatsoever is used and

applied to prolong the life of man, is dull, dead, and
of no force.

The Anatomy of Melancholy, Second Partition, pp. 123–24

Now, however, the real culprit was holding up her hand: the
depression murder case had been given its most important
lead so far.

In depression I'd often get the fact of a situation right but
the pronouns wrong. I'd relive other people's rejection of
me and their refusal to support my creativity. Every time
I reproached someone else, however, it covered my act of
self-neglect. If that weren't the case, nobody could hurt
me in the first place. What really hurts is your own self-
abandonment: once you've started the process, you can hardly
blame other people for following your lead. But nobody can
force you to consent to anything like this against your will.

If you were to abandon a child as often as I've abandoned
myself you'd soon be in prison and a pariah. Staying with
myself when I don't know what's going on has always been
my difficulty, as if I had an allergic reaction to the void at
the centre of myself.

Even depression can't hurt you, unless you take it as a
form of permission to kick yourself in the teeth. Learn to
treat yourself kindly, though, and it could and should change
your life.

*

A monk asked Master Haryo, 'What is the way?'
Haryo said, 'A realised man falling into the well.'

From the Book of Miscellaneous Koans
used by the Sanbo Kyodan Zendo

Trying to control emotions is like attempting to balance on a ball – it's just not possible and you look a fool while doing it. You have to learn to fall, to make a practice of it, because that's the condition of the world. After all, what's dancing but falling gracefully? Once you know that standing up isn't an option, you can learn to love falling.

In my diary, that autumn, I scribbled down a stray hunch: 'Wonder if surfing would be good for depression – just being thrown around by a force greater than yourself for a while?'

I was coming up to forty, a traditional time for taking stock. What hadn't I done in my life? The first thing was owning a pair of leather trousers. That was easily remedied.

The second thing was learning to surf.

*

Glossary

POP UP – The single motion of standing up on your surfboard, from belly to feet.

SWELL – The marching lines of wind-inspired energy that travel across the open water, crest and make waves in shallow water.

WHITE WATER – The broken or spent part of a wave that has peaked and toppled over.

WIPE OUT – Falling off your surfboard.

Doug Werner, *Surfer's Start-Up: A Beginner's Guide to Surfing*, (Tracks, Chula Vista, 1993), pp. 100–101

Although it was, by now, the beginning of November, I found a surf school that was still teaching in Llangennith, one of the Gower's finest surf beaches. The school turned out to be an empty container, where we changed into damp wetsuits, an intensely unpleasant feeling. We were each given a surfboard, like a personal headstone to carry down to the beach. I was still so weak after months in bed that David, the instructor, had to help me with mine.

I asked David, who was shockingly young, how we could judge which waves were good to surf, expecting an existential answer. 'Ones with white on top,' he replied, which meant every single one that day. That would teach me to be poetic. We were given a quick lesson on the sand, told how to catch a wave and then how to stand 'in one swift, graceful movement' on the board. Then we headed out towards the breakers.

My first wave caught me entirely by surprise. I know that, technically, I caught it, but I was astonished by the strength of its push as it propelled me forward. I managed to kneel on my surfboard and shot into the shallows, whooping.

There were leaden skies and monsoon downpours, but we couldn't have cared less. We lost sight of the Worm's Head peninsula because of the rain, but we were so intent on surfing that we had little interest in the view. The falling was lovely. We were told: If you fall underneath your board, don't be in too much of a hurry to get up. Count a couple of beats and you'll come up a few feet away and it won't hit you on the head.

The water drove up hard into my ears when I fell, but it was fantastic to be out there, in the tumult, equipped with the discipline to deal with it. Then the sun came out and in stained-glass light I looked across at my fellow surfers. Wet-suits must be the sporting equivalent of a dinner jacket: they made everyone look great. We gleamed like seals. We all leant into the sea, as if on a slope, guiding our surfboards gently at our sides. We were heroic, like Soviet statues in a socialist wind, each one going out to meet their fate, to brave destruction.

Then I managed to stand up for a couple of seconds. I was surfing, poised across the wave, falling beautifully, moving without effort. The ride was absolutely smooth, though I was standing on chaos. It was like surfing down shiny polished stairs, the ground moving beneath you.

And for a moment, I was that paradoxical thing, a moving statue, scattering spray, the sun down my shiny flank, weather in my hair and me moving from one second to the next, totally in balance. Then I fell back again into the roaring wave.

That night, still happy, back in the shack, I felt a drop of sea water warmed by my ear trickle onto my pillow. It was like a secret told to me alone, the most tender secret.

This previous year had been arid and difficult but, at the same time, in its midst, I'd felt a completeness and freedom that was totally new. For the first time, I was fully present in my own life, not distracted. And I wouldn't trade that for anything, not even health.

CHAPTER TEN

A Reliable Witness

I thought that, once I'd sobered up, I'd have no trouble becoming a reliable witness in my own case. Knowing yourself, however, takes more work than this. As you explore deeper towards the seabed, the monsters that loom out at you from the dark become stranger and more disconcerting. We all have an in-built censorship system which allows us to face our greatest fears only when we're ready for them.

Staying sober, though difficult, was a huge step in the right direction. My quality of life began to improve immediately. I lost weight, began to sleep well and even started to giggle again, which sounded strange to me at first. A few months later Leighton and I started seeing each other. It was an unlikely combination – a 53-year-old 'hairy-arsed ex-boatswain' and a poet finishing off her doctorate – but somehow, we never stopped laughing. I began to cheer up because, as I said to Leighton, 'It's amazing how much having your bum bitten in private gives you confidence in public.'

One day, there was a wasp in the office. With a telephone directory, I carefully manoeuvred it out of the window. It had spent hours butting its head against the window glass, baffled by being able to see the day outside but unable to reach it. Suddenly a window had opened for me too. I'd been let out into the sun, able to live a life I'd only been able to watch before.

Staying happy takes work and this maintenance has to be done even when things are going well – perhaps, most especially when you're out of immediate danger. When I came back to Cardiff I was lucky enough to be referred to a consultant psychiatrist who also practised as a psychotherapist. He was to be Sherlock Holmes to my Dr Watson for the next decade and more, as I tried to piece together a realistic picture of what had happened. This was a difficult case of detection because at the beginning all I knew was that I felt terrible and wanted to drink. If there was a body to be found and identified, I had no idea where to start looking.

Over the years we seemed to spiral endlessly over the same old stories, obsessions and difficulties. It must have been excruciatingly boring but my psychiatrist was never anything less than totally attentive. He asked good questions, stayed quiet when he had nothing to say and was invariably helpful and realistic in his suggestions about how to look at old situations. When I announced, very excitedly one week, that I was engaged, he paused and then asked 'To whom?', even though I'd been with Leighton for years. This question still makes me laugh because I used to be so impulsive that he was quite right to take nothing for granted.

Slowly, over the years, I was able to separate what I felt had happened to me from the actual situations in which

I'd been. For example, I began to see that far from being a failure – as I felt – that I'd actually chosen the life I was now living. Even though I had no confidence in my own judgement, and even though it felt all wrong, my life in Cardiff was now suiting me very well. I was in a city I really liked, away from the stresses and dangers of places like New York and Oxford. I was earning a living and, best of all, I was with someone I was crazy about without feeling crazy. In short, far from being a disaster, my life was beginning to be right for me.

This is not to say that I found making myself at home easy. In fact, it required me to revisit all the issues which had driven me away in the first place. I thought to begin with that I was only touching base before flitting off again on my travels. I told Leighton to make the most of me because I was only planning to be in Cardiff for a year. I argued the case out in my notebook:

> Staying at home is the hardest thing.
> Then travel!
> How do I know that this is home?
> Home is boring.
> So is travel. Stay.

Gradually, therapy helped me to put my life in perspective and to see that the damage I'd done to myself with my feelings of guilt was out of all proportion to what had actually happened. I discovered that my worst fear was that I had somehow 'ruined' R's life by doing what I wanted to and was able to see that this was very far from being the case. I also began to learn how to draw a line between my mother's depressions and my own. 'You are not responsible for your mother,' the psychiatrist told me firmly. She and I slowly got to know each other again and, once I'd stopped drinking, I felt that our relationship was on a different and much better footing. At last, I was beginning to know where I was.

At one point I decided that I'd go back to the drink in a big way. Somehow, however, I was able to think the process through. I knew that something had gone wrong in my emotional life, and that this was what prompted me to abandon myself. I began to interrogate myself at various ages, asking did I want to go back on the pop? The answer was 'Yes' each time until I reached the age seven, when I wanted, at last, to stay with myself. I decided that I liked myself at that age, so I stayed on the wagon and the crisis passed.

This matter of staying with myself was helped greatly by my taste for hats. In the middle of that first January home I went out one lunchtime and bought a wide-brimmed 1920s-style hat with a navy blue velvet band in the sale. It was an instant success and elicited admiring comments immediately as I strutted back to the office.

A hat is a help in gathering your thoughts because it's a sartorial way of saying 'You Are Here'. It's the arrow that leads to yourself on the map, the start of finding your own way home. It gave me added height and presence, made me feel a little hyper-real. It helped me to learn that even if people didn't want to release me I could act unilaterally and let them go. It made me feel responsible for my own life, capable of action. The irony of a hat is that it makes you feel as though you're hiding your identity while, in fact, you're even more conspicuous than usual. This particular hat curved over my brow most elegantly and meant that my view of the world was only partial. Existentially this is accurate but because this brim possessed a certain line, it was also stylish. It made me feel that I could leave at any time, because I already had a hat onto which I could hold.

Poetry soon began to stir in me. I realised that, if I was to go back to writing, it would have to be in the spirit in which I began, aged seven. Writing went wrong for me whenever I mixed it up with gaining prestige for myself or pleasing others. I'd have to go back to an earlier self, to just sitting quietly at a dining table, playing with words, in a humming, contented child-like way. One night I sat up suddenly in bed to catch a ball that someone had thrown me in my dream. I knew from then that something creative was going to happen.

My great fear was that I'd never be able to write sober because I'd now become too dull and boring. I was making a common mistake among writers – confusing chaos with creativity. Of course, you can manage the odd piece of good work in the middle of a crisis – a fluke – but this is the exception rather than the rule. The truth is, it's far easier to lead a colourful, 'poetic' life than actually to write poems. The former requires a good liver and seedy friends, the latter all the discipline of a civil servant. Poets with even a small amount of talent have to choose between the two lifestyles periodically, if not for good. Do you want to act out the life of a poet (booze, friends, funny anecdotes, 'what a great laugh')? Or do you want to write poems ('Sorry, I can't come out to play, I'm writing')? I had tried the former for a long time and had failed, been fired. It was time to give the second lifestyle a go.

My notebook showed how quickly I started to notice the world:

> Worked in the morning. Found a tortoise in the alley on my way out, a huge thing, its head like a glans popping out of its foreskin. Picked it up, put it in a box. Gave it lettuce, which it ate rapaciously. Its pink tongue was unexpected, like the pink of a black man's palm. It belongs to a house round the corner, to a blind man.

Then, one night, I got up and found myself scribbling in the dark, as I used to do when I was a child, jotting down words and rhymes. Suddenly I felt sane again and was able to go back to sleep.

The signs were good but still I was unable to write a poem. It was as if I was learning to write again with my left hand, having been switched to the right in school – it was taking a long time to re-learn my natural stroke. In February, things came to a head. I remember praying and saying, 'OK, if this is how it's meant to be, that's fine. If you don't want me to write, that's fine, I'll learn to live without it.' That night, I wrote a thirty-line Valentine poem for Leighton full of lovely dirty rhymes. Since then, I haven't looked back: the problem has been finding the time to work on all my ideas, rather than coping with writer's block.

This time round writing felt like a completely different

activity, because my motives were so different. Far from being something that was driving me mad, a Fury, it became a powerful weapon for sanity. A. R. Luria wrote in *Mind of a Mnemonist* that there are two kinds of imagination:

> We know that a creative imagination – the kind of imagination that makes for great inventors – operates in a manner that is closely in touch with reality. But there is another type of imagination whose activity is not directed toward the external world, but is nourished by desire and becomes a substitute for action by making action seem pointless.

This distinction describes exactly the difference between the way the drunk sits in a fug, feeling brilliant and poetic, talking nonsense, and the hard graft of actual writing, which judges itself not by internal standards but by the degree to which it reflects outside reality. This is as far from being an intellectual matter as can be, because the second type of imagination is life-giving and the first can kill you.

The reason why writing is so hard and frightening is that, ironically, the process requires you to abandon your fictions and face up to your own truths. If you don't do this, the form you choose will show you up as a liar. Poetry is much like a child in this: if it catches you lying, it will expose you. I tried to write some 'victim' poems: they were terrible. I decided I wanted revenge, so I wrote some rants. These were even worse. Once I'd got over my pique, however, I made a thrilling discovery. What works in poetry is the truth. Bullshit snarls the whole process up. Fortunately, poetry follows the soul and not the will.

It was only then that I began to realise how arrogant I'd been to question this gift in the first place. After all, what was the alternative? Being depressed and drunk. Instead of moaning about what wanting to write had cost me, I should be grateful for another chance. I knew now that this had nothing at all to do with Doing Well or being a successful writer. The gift was the activity itself, like being shown how to use a dowsing rod, except that instead of looking for water I was divining what was real in my life.

I had thought, for a long time, that I had a choice between being human and being a poet. Now I knew that being a poet is my best way of being human. When I finally realised that it's not a question of either one or the other, I cried with relief.

But where does depression fit into this? It's essential to writing if, by depression, you mean the feeling of not knowing the meaning of anything, of not having energy at your own beck and call, of falling without control in the world. In order to 'catch' a poem you have to be prepared to write nonsense for quite a period. You need to look at the world out of focus for a while in order to see it in a new, fresh way when it finally resolves into a clear image. Without this obscurity, a poem is likely to be facile, the product of the conscious brain rather than the record of a journey into the unconscious and back. This not knowing, far from being an enemy to writing, is the guarantor of its quality. It should, therefore, be cherished and not endured, valued rather than avoided at all costs.

The same is true of everyday life. After all, our lives are

the most important work of art any of us produce – including poets – and they take just as much labour, discipline and craft as any other creation. In life I had become addicted to 'up' and would do anything to avoid the inevitable, corresponding 'down'. One woman describes her depression as 'tending the void'. For a while she has to concentrate on the emptiness she feels, pay it its due, then she can come back to the company of her family and friends. I like this phrase's almost religious respect towards depression. The void can be tended, gardened almost. It's only bad if you're frightened of it. If you're not, it is a fertile place – the start of everything you know next.

Our bodies live out our metaphors in illness, as if they were instinctive poets. For example if, like me, you're greedy and drink too much, you get addicted and then you really learn what Too Much can do. Then, if you're lucky, you are able to have second thoughts. Or, you feel as though you want to do More all the time. The body decides to give you doing nothing: total depression. 'How do you like that? You hate it? Yes, but pay attention. This nothing is achieving far, far more than all your frantic running about. When you were hyperactive you were just repeating the same futile actions time and time again. Stand still for a while and notice how you're transformed, let's do some real work for a change.'

*

I've already outlined some of the long-term emotional habits that have made me prone to depression and the genetic element to the disorder. Neither of these would have kicked in, however, unless a particular short-term crisis had catapulted me into clinical depression. I'll outline the events which acted as triggers for me – because they show how the whole mechanism of depression works, and how it can be wiser than ourselves.

After a few years in independent television, I went to work as a producer at BBC Wales. I finished my thesis, a publisher offered me a contract, but I decided I couldn't bear to spend another second on the blasted thing, so I put the essay on the most obscure bookshelf in the house and happily forgot about it. I wrote as much poetry as I could in my spare time and eventually published books in Welsh and then in English.

I was promoted at work and eventually accepted an administrative job as Chief Assistant to the Controller of BBC Wales (with my own office, which was very handy for scribbling when I shouldn't be). I was often away at weekends doing readings; I took holidays to allow me to read further afield in the United States or at the Sydney Writers' Festival. I juggled a great deal and seemed to be running two careers successfully. The more I did, the more I seemed able to do. When I wanted to write, I'd get up early, do a few hours before going into the office at nine, so that the BBC didn't get all my best concentration.

In the meantime, Leighton and I had reached an important decision about children. By 1998 we'd been married for about five years and I was at that stage in my thirties when you Have to Decide. Leighton had had a vasectomy nearly twenty years previously, so we decided to investigate a reversal. We went to see an urologist in Bristol who felt Leighton's tubes, declared that he could reverse the procedure surgically but that the chance of a baby after so long was 97% against. We booked Leighton in for the operation and went home.

My cold feet began with the rectal shave. Even though we were paying a fortune for the operation, the hospital wanted Leighton to turn up hairless. When I refused to do it, it started me thinking: if I wasn't willing to give him a rectal shave, was I really prepared for the sacrifices having children would involve?

There's nothing like the prospect of having your loved one's giblets operated on – perhaps needlessly – to focus your mind on procreation. That evening and the following morning we talked the whole issue through again and decided against it. This came as a huge surprise to me because I'd always assumed, without question, that I would want children at all costs. Because this was not the decision I expected, it somehow seemed more real because it wasn't feeding my fantasies about being a Successful Human Being, with a child at my breast and a poetry book in the other hand. Leighton's age was against us and he already had grown-up children and even a granddaughter. If we were going to start another family, financially I would have to commit myself to working at the BBC for the next twenty years, to crèches and cramming my writing into the gaps. This wasn't a life that I could see our marriage being able to sustain, especially as Leighton had deep reservations about his own ability to cope with children in his sixties. We had made a commitment to each other before God, so our decision had to be made on the grounds of what was right for our marriage, and for both of us.

We cancelled the operation. Leighton was ecstatic with relief and only after we'd decided showed how unhappy he would have been if I'd wanted to go ahead with having children, though he would have been willing to do it, for my sake. I was relieved because a decision that had been hanging over us almost since we met had been taken, and a crucial area of our life had been resolved.

I expected to feel great because we had been brave enough to make the decision but, as time went on, I felt worse and worse. I told myself that I should be glad that I was now free to do anything I wanted but that didn't help. I began to wonder if we'd made the wrong decision. Any decision about reproduction strikes at your very core and a huge amount of social pressure equates motherhood with virtue, caricaturing childless women as calculating, selfish harridans. Our decision had nothing to do with my writing poetry, and certainly wasn't a sacrifice I was prepared to make in order to lead an artist's life. Any decision made on those grounds would be monstrous, guaranteed to scupper any chance of being a decent person, let alone a good writer. For me the choice between motherhood and writing was heavily loaded because of my past. The issues the decision raised were very confusing to me and I ended up feeling like an immoral, hurtful and unacceptable human being.

Around the same time Sister Elaine, who was pleased with my progress in meditation, said I could tackle a five-day retreat. I had already taken a couple of two-day sessions in my stride. But this was the first since we cancelled Leighton's operation, and I was in for a much bumpier ride. Of course the five days in silent meditation brought all my emotions out into the open, because there was nowhere left to hide – no meetings to go to, no articles to write and certainly no way of being carried away by external or internal lies. The first two days of the retreat went relatively well, except that every time I went to see Sister Elaine, I'd burst into tears. I didn't think too much of this because I'm a bit of a weeper anyway but it was annoying that I didn't have any tissues on me, because I was never expecting the floods of tears.

By the end of the third day, however, I knew that I'd crashed. I camped outside the Roshi's study after tea and waited till Sister Elaine came out, and told her that I had to leave, that I was going mad. She didn't question my decision but said, 'OK, but why don't you go for a walk to calm yourself down? And stay for supper, because you shouldn't drive without having something to eat.'

Even before I'd left the room I knew I'd been had by a good one and that I would end up staying for the rest of the retreat. I was put on 'light duties', one sit in every three, and spent the rest of the time in the garden. On the last day, I rejoined the group and was able to follow the usual schedule.

It was then that, for some reason I can't fathom, I suddenly felt a peace so complete that it made everything all right. I hadn't changed – I was still aware of feeling shaky, confused and tormented – but in the midst of it all, I experienced the best ten minutes of my life. This peace, which couldn't have come from me, didn't blot anything out, in fact all my problems were still there, but they didn't have any power to hurt, they were part of a perfection so complete that they only needed to be left alone in it. It was only ten minutes but it was proof. Once you've had a taste of peace, nothing else will satisfy.

I went home after the end of the retreat looking awful but feeling on top of the world. Leighton was furious that I hadn't come home when I began to feel bad but I couldn't persuade him that what I knew now was worth all that sitting. What I'd had was proof that my own thoughts and obsessions couldn't harm me if I accepted them for what they were – no more than a form of internal weather. This was to stand me in very good stead in the months of depression to come.

It wasn't long until I crashed for real. All it took was a little more exhaustion, the finishing of a very difficult book and a casual comment about feeding only the pregnant sheep on a farm. The day before I finally stopped, I woke up knowing that I was in big trouble. It wasn't that I was just tired – although I was – my blood felt all wrong. I knew I'd no more energy to run away from what had been bothering me. Depression was about to take the whole matter out of my hands and to show me another, better way of coming to terms with myself. I had to grieve for the life I was never going to have without children. The adjustment required in your expectations and view of yourself, particularly in relation to time, is huge. Part of the work of my depression was, I'm sure, to allow me to get used to this new reality. A number of female friends who had been in the same position as me announced that they were pregnant. I was pleased that I wasn't in the least envious. I'm now a doting step-grandmother and godmother.

I was about to be shown how to put down burdens I'd been carrying for too long and how to leave that baggage there. I was to be re-taught the basics of living in such a way that the poisons of judgmentalism and envy which had been tormenting me would be burnt out of my system. 'Leave it to me,' the Depression said. 'I'll take over now.'

CHAPTER ELEVEN

Dos in Depression

The most important advice I can give to anyone suffering from depression is to find a doctor and/or psychiatrist who understands depression and to whom you can talk openly. Run a mile from anyone who doesn't take depression seriously, or who seems to want to get rid of you or to shut you up. Finding good treatment for depression can be a matter of life and death. At the very least it can make the difference between living fully, despite depression, or needlessly enduring its endless cyclical miseries.

1 Remember that depression can't harm you

Even though depression's hell to go through, try to remember that, although it hurts, it actually can't harm you. Dealing with depression can resolve issues that were out of reach before you became ill. Thus, it may, in the long term, improve your life, if you can bear the short-term agony. I repeat: depression itself can't harm you, only what *you* do about it can.

It's not the people who get depressed who go mad, it's those who don't. Those who experience its emotional short circuit have a chance to check the wiring throughout the house and prevent the start of a fatal electrical fire. People who listen to depression's instructions stand an excellent chance of recovering and staying well.

What does depression teach? It taught a perfectionist like me that, even stripped down and humiliated by the lack of any kind of spark or graciousness, I was able to endure. Even though I was unrecognisable, I survived as a human being and showed a basic self-loyalty of which I had thought myself incapable. Depression's gifts are dark but very precious.

Even though you'd do anything to make yourself feel better, part of the recovery is learning that you can't. With this disease, you have to go along with being ill for as long as is necessary for your inner transformation to be established sufficiently well for your resurrection not to be a false revival. Rilke knew the importance of accepting illness when he wrote:

> If some aspect of your life is not well, then consider the illness to be the means for an organism to free itself from something foreign to it. In that case you must help it to be ill and to have its whole illness, to let it break out. That is the course of its progress.
>
> So much is happening within you at present, dear Mr Kappus. You need to be as patient as one ill and as optimistic as one recuperating, for perhaps you are both.   *Letters to a Young Poet*, p. 86

After months of being ill and of thinking of my depression as a sign of utter failure on my part, it suddenly occurred to me that the opposite was true. My illness was, in fact, a sign of success. My body and mind had delivered me a breathing space which I would never consciously have permitted myself. They had given me a chance to relinquish old ideas and experiences which had been exhausting me and time to adjust to new facts about my life. I was being helped to get real again. It was a maternity leave without the baby, a writer's bursary without the need to produce a book.

Depression isn't the same as despair, though it's easy to confuse the two. Depression's more like desolation, being alone in an uninhabited place. This isolation is the first step in self-knowledge, and the internal desert makes such learning a matter of survival. Distinctions, such as this one made by Simone Weil, become crucial: 'Human misery is not created by the extreme affliction that falls upon some human beings, it is only revealed by it.' (*The Notebooks of Simone Weil*, Vol I, p. 262.) That is, it's not you who have created this misery, it's just an aspect of how life is. Depression's useful because it shows you clearly your true condition, and gives you a chance to change what can be changed. The rest you have to accept.

2 Remember that depression always ends

As an illness, depression is very self-effacing. Its purpose is to teach you how to avoid having to become depressed again. In that sense, depression is a very kind disorder, and will return only if you refuse to learn the lessons it has to teach you.

Even without medication or psychotherapy, depression is often recurrent but will, almost invariably, right itself. The trick is to try and remember in the middle of a bout that this will end. The fact that it is almost impossible to believe in the middle of a down that you can ever feel differently makes it even more important that you try. Your life may depend on your remembering this. Have a checklist of depression's main symptoms handy, to remind yourself of the distinction between you and the disease. Without scrutiny depression makes you feel so terrible that you conclude immediately that you're just a lazy, good-for-nothing malingerer, a dreadful person. Feeling low, being unable to get out of bed, sleeping too much, lacking concentration and hating your life are all symptoms of depression and not character traits. A true malingerer would never reproach him or herself with being useless, because the real skivers hide their own failings from their conscious minds. You just have to remind yourself all the time that you're not evil but that you're ill.

There is an innate buoyancy in depression and you need to learn to float in it. This isn't a property that you can perceive in the normal fashion, because your usual energy source has dried up. It's a life that seeps in through the dark, without your knowing about it. This internal landscape looks like a desert but all the life of the savannah is there, if only you'll let it take root and grow.

3 Listen to what depression is telling you, and change your life accordingly

This is where you need to turn detective. Your depression is the most important case of your life: you must probe, agitate and investigate until the whole sordid story is out in the open. If you weren't ashamed of it you wouldn't have hidden it in the first place. This may take a long time, and psychotherapy or therapy may be necessary. For, as it says in the Gnostic gospel of Thomas:

> If you bring forth what is within you, what you bring
> forth will save you. If you do not bring forth what
> is within you, what you do not bring forth will
> destroy you.

Your mission is to find out what needs to change in your life and to change it. The depression itself will drop you huge hints. For example: What does the illness itself stop you from doing? For me the main things were: going to work; thinking too much, being hyperactive; and not having enough fun. What does the illness force you to do in order to recover? Waste time, read silly magazines, watch trash on the telly, go walking, take easy exercise, forgive someone, leave the past behind. This is your most promising lead: the symptoms of depression actually show you, in themselves, how to get better.

How can you hear what depression is trying to tell you? The language we have to learn to understand depression isn't a verbal one. You post a question with your actions and listen for your body's response. For example, I went back to work too quickly, despite the doctor's warnings. Very soon I began to feel unwell again. One by one, my symptoms started flooding back, depression's way of saying, 'No, stupid, I told you not to do this work. You're not listening . . .' The symptoms intensified and, in no time, I was ill enough to start taking them seriously again.

Make sure that any cross you're carrying is your own, not someone else's. Make sure that you are feeling bad about things that are real, not fictions, either yours or made up by other people trying to avoid their own guilt. Above all, depression is a disease that is concerned with authenticity. Reality and realism in how you live your life is far more trustworthy than how you feel emotionally. That is likely to change from day to day; proving forever that how you feel about something isn't a true reflection of the facts. For example, I vacillated a great deal about our decision on children. One day I'd feel bereft and full of grief, the next relieved that I was still free to please myself. I began to feel worse and worse, not better. The only thing that helped me to move on was acknowledging that, however much pain and grief it cost me, it was a decision based on the reality of our situation. This was the only ground on which I could have any peace about the issue, so it had to be the right one. As it turned out, even in the midst of feeling horrifically low, I still was never tempted to change the big decision we'd made about Leighton's vasectomy.

4 However much you blame other people, depression will only take you back to yourself

Forgeries sometimes tell the truth, though they're not authentic in themselves. Iolo Morganwg, an eighteenth-century poet pretending to be the Bards of Ancient Britain wrote:

> Three things which a man ought to do with his heart: to feel it; to teach it; and to fear it.
>
> *Barddas: Bardism*, tr. Rev. J. Williams
> (Welsh MS. Society), I. p. 305

The heart is to be feared because it doesn't always tell the truth. No matter how you've been mistreated by other people, if you follow depression's clues honestly, the culprit will always be yourself. This is a fine and fortunate thing, because many people's lives are ruined by having unworthy enemies. In depression's case, you and your enemy are always perfectly matched.

The monster at the middle of the labyrinth in which you've been lost is never a stranger, but an old, old friend. In your nightmares, the person who's been frightening you is yourself. Without depression I'm quite sure that I would never have had the courage to leave the daylight behind and rely on a frail thread of sanity to guide me back. In the last resort, you see that, far from being the prey of monsters with an objective existence, you've been scaring yourself silly in the dark with spooks of your own making.

And of course the monster in the middle of the maze isn't heroic but always ridiculous. It only has dignity as long as you're too afraid to look at it. Once recognised, it's comic rather than horrific. If you're not too proud to suffer this humiliation – that the reason you've been putting off living your real life is, at base, foolish – then you will never have to face up to anything worse. I had, over the years, become used to thinking of myself as a perfectionist Tragic Queen. In order to make this true and prove that I wasn't the bitch I thought I was, I was quite prepared – no, driven – to follow a career I didn't want, to have children for the wrong reasons and not to do the one thing that gives me more pleasure than anything else. Far from being heroic, this self-denial was just phoney and more than a little silly.

In one of our sessions, my psychiatrist asked how things would be if I could be as perfect as I said I wanted to be. I told him about a gravestone in Cathays graveyard in Cardiff. Last resting-place of many of the city's bourgeois, this garden of rest has a grave which boasts: 'He wore the white flower of a blameless life'. 'Fine', he said, 'that's perfectionism; but could you ever take such a person seriously?'

The answer is, of course, no, because almost invariably what we think we want is ridiculous. It's not as if trying to be a perfectionist stopped me from falling flat on my face. I don't want to live a blameless life, I want to live a real one. So now my emotional ambitions have changed. I'd like to live a life in which I make lots of mistakes. It is probably much safer than trying not to make them and definitely more fun.

5 Learn how to distinguish between your rubbish and what's true

Depression is an extreme existential situation, a civil war between your ego and your soul, between how your willpower would like you to live and the life that would really suit you. The ego believes that, even, in the middle of depression's devastation, it can still cut a deal. Depression teaches you that the only permanent way out is by finding and accepting the truths you have been avoiding, even if you thought you'd already faced them. A relapse shows that you haven't and that there's more work to be done.

6 Hints for discernment

a) When does a particular idea or obsession take hold? Is it when you're feeling relaxed and contented? Or does it visit you in the tumult of an emotional low, when you have a crisis of spirits? Trust the first, distrust the second.

Some years I make a rough list of what I'd like to achieve in the year ahead – to finish a book of poems, to do some house maintenance, to get a little fitter, to take more time off. One crucial year I noticed that, despite being thirty-eight, I'd left 'have a baby' off my list. I wasn't harried when I drew up that list, so the omission was a significant and very telling clue to what I really wanted, though I wasn't yet willing to accept what it meant.

On the other hand, the 'I'm a monster because I don't

have children' thought usually comes to me in the middle of a low. This is like accusing the seaweed thrown up on a beach during a storm of causing the gale itself, just because every time there's a storm it's there. I now know that this is totally inaccurate and that the baby reproach isn't the cause but a consequence of the tumult. One of the best insights in Dante's *Divine Comedy* comes when he writes that God's 'will is our peace'. It confirms that when a thing is right, I feel calm and relaxed. It's only when I'm trying to persuade myself that something that's wrong is actually right that I tie myself in knots.

b) Does the idea allow you to take it or leave it, without punishing you, does it grant you free will? Or does it insist that it's the only way you're ever going to be happy, and that your whole life will be ruined unless you act on this impulse immediately?

I used to be prone to Spring Fever, the feeling that you could fall in love with anybody and everybody (it lasts an afternoon and then it's gone). The fever works this way: you're convinced that you're destined for a certain man, and that your life will only be on course if you run away with him. Half an hour later, you remember another man and are seized by the idea that it's *him* you really love. If you look at the situation, though, it can't be love, as it purports to be, because the men in question are interchangeable. Real love is man-specific; craving is general. Spring fever is only your own restlessness looking for an object.

c) How many 'shoulds', 'musts' and 'oughts' are in how you're talking to yourself?

If there are several, you are hounding yourself with a pre-ordained agenda, rather than calmly observing yourself. 'I should do it,' means, 'I don't really feel like doing it but I'll consider myself a terrible failure/ wimp/ bitch if I don't'. This is a mode of thinking which doesn't allow you to dissent, it's totalitarian. Even if you do manage to force yourself to marry someone, go to the gym or quit smoking on these grounds, you will only be able to keep it up by sheer willpower because it's not something that you really want to do, and willpower alone always fails.

d) Learn to trust the first thought and to dismiss the second.

Very often the problem isn't the content of our thoughts but in the links we make between them. Often my second thought presumes too much. The first thought is not only more accurate but usually more humble than its brainy but tricksy successor. For example, as I was feeling a lot better one day, I found myself thinking, 'I'm so happy today', followed closely by 'If only Mam were this happy'. I was shocked when I noticed how automatically I was willing to compromise my own wellbeing by making it conditional on someone else's. Besides, how do I know at any given time that my mother is not happy? And even if she isn't, what business is it of mine? Once I told my mother that all I wanted was for her to be happy. 'What if I'm not a happy type of person?' she said, perfectly reasonably. If I want the freedom to live my own life for myself, then I have to allow it to everyone else.

e) Let go of what things mean.

I've already shown how dodgy a depressive's thoughts can be: 'If I get myself a new house, then that will mean that I'm a success/good person.' No it won't.

All we can reasonably do is to live our lives – their significance is none of our business. The meaning of the whole is God's department – indeed, that meaning is partly what He is, but this is hidden from us. To pretend to know the meaning of everything is to lead a narrow, fundamentalist life. How much better to watch things as they appear, rather than as we might wish to codify them – certainly better for an artist, who has to resist all kinds of propaganda, especially his or her own.

In one of the best passages of *The Anatomy of Melancholy*, Burton advises depressives on how best to repel such devilish thoughts without hating themselves even more and thus becoming too mixed up in them:

> Therefore be not overmuch troubled and dismayed with such kind of suggestions, at least if they please thee not, because they are not thy personal sins, for which thou shalt incur the wrath of God, or His displeasure: contemn, neglect them, let them go as they come, strive not too violently, or trouble thyself too much, but as our Saviour said to Satan in like case, say thou, 'Avoid, Satan,' I detest thee and them. *Satanae est mala ingerere* (saith Austin), *nostrum non consentire*: as Satan labours to suggest, so must we strive not to give consent, and it will be sufficient: the more anxious and solicitous thou art, the more perplexed, the more thou shalt otherwise be troubled and entangled.
>
> *op cit*, Third Partition, p. 418

The devil is always pretending that he knows what things mean, because sin is a refusal to become who we really are, settling for less than God intended us to be. In this case, Satan's just another way of talking about the way we lie to ourselves. After all, what are the depressive's self-hating thoughts but a falsification of what he or she really is when well?

f) Make the most of this depression.

Once you're over your horror at being depressed, try to forget that it's a negative thing and live it as fully as possible.

On my first visit to London when I was ten, my parents took us on the Big Dipper at the Battersea Funfair. By the time the carriage came to a halt I was nearly hysterical with fear and vowed I'd never go on a rollercoaster again. I haven't been on one physically, but I haven't had my wish, because depression's plunges can be just as frightening.

But look how the men in charge have lost their fear of the ups and downs, and can stand, perfectly relaxed on the moving ride. I'll never like big dippers of any description, but I think I'm training myself to move with the carriages. When you're not screaming as you come to the top of the slope, the view from the summit can be very unusual.

Losing your fear of depression is very liberating because it allows you to see it as a way of being trained in reality. For, as Robert Pirsig wrote in *Zen and the Art of Motorcycle Maintenance*, 'stuckness' isn't

> the worst of all possible situations, but the best possible situation you could be in. After all, it's exactly

this stuckness that Zen Buddhists go to so much trouble to induce; through koans, deep breathing, sitting still and the like. Your mind is empty, you have a 'hollow-flexible' attitude of 'beginner's mind'. You're right at the front end of the train of knowledge, at the track of reality itself. Consider, for a change, that this is a moment to be not feared but to be cultivated. If your mind is truly, profoundly stuck, then you may be much better off than when it is loaded with ideas . . .

Stuckness shouldn't be avoided. It's the physic predecessor of all real understanding.

Robert M. Pirsig, *Zen and the Art of Motorcycle Maintenance*,
(Bantam, 1979), p. 279

The key here is being fully present in any experience, pleasant or otherwise. For a chronic flitter like me, this is a great antidote to self-abandonment. After all, if you can accept your depression so completely that you even enjoy it (but without wishing to prolong it) then isn't that a kind of perfection?

g) Look at how you're doing things, as well as what you're doing.

Depression is as much a disease of *how* you do things as of *what* you're doing. No matter how right something may be for you, you can pursue it with a fanaticism which changes that boon into a burden. I still find it very difficult not to overdo things. My head wants to do everything, but my body's wiser. I'm learning not to over-commit myself socially and work-wise. My depression thermostat is turned on very low at the moment, and cuts in at the least sign of strain, forcing me to cancel over-ambitious plans and to rest. Under depression's guidance, I'm in danger of becoming a sensible person. I can't take the credit for this new maturity, because, all too often, I still have to be forced to live within my energy means, until I learn the lesson properly.

h) Pace yourself.

Because you're suffering from a serious energy deficit, you need to take a totally new look at which activities leave you in the red. For the moment, you're like a rosebush, which only has a limited amount of vigorous growth in it before its branches become wan and straggly. At this stage in your recovery, pruning back the demands you make on yourself ruthlessly is the best way of restoring you to your usual thorny self.

Your energy audit may not correspond to other people's assessment of 'what's good for an invalid'. Indeed, you may find that your own conclusions are surprising. A visit from an aunt who has your wellbeing at heart but who's an energy thief leaves you dispirited. Stop her from coming round for a while. Exercise is hard to do but gives you a lift. Keep doing it. No matter how much other people think that going out with the girls will 'take you out of yourself', if you hate the idea, postpone it.

The way to think of it is like this: you used to be able to afford to pay your energy bills quarterly. Now you've fallen on harder times and you have to feed the meter, pay as you go. This situation won't last forever, but is necessary in your current austerity. There will be plenty of time later to set up a direct debit arrangement, after you've learnt how to live within your energy budget.

i) Keep a mood chart.

My psychiatrist gave me a mood chart so that I could track how I felt from week to week. I was allowed to choose my own categories – which ranged from 'totally debilitated' through 'a bit down' and 'bright' to 'very happy' – which I then plotted on a graph, with one mark for each day. At the end of the month, I'd join the dots and see what kind of month it had been.

The early months were below the Normal line so often that you'd have sworn the patient was dead, and in many ways I was. As I kept the chart for longer and longer, the patterns became a very useful way of checking how I thought I was against an objective pattern. Sometimes, when I thought that I'd had a bad month, the graph showed that it was more positive than I'd remembered.

This type of graph, used with the help of a psychiatrist, can be very helpful in deciding the right dose of anti-depressants. After improving slowly but steadily for nine months on Seroxat, I suddenly and inexplicably went through a prolonged mood dip. Because I was keeping the chart, we could see that this was uncharacteristic and, with my GP, came to the conclusion that a new drug needed to be pre-scribed. This sometimes happens for no apparent reason, so we switched to an alternative anti-depressant called Venlafax-ine. It was most reassuring to watch the mood-line creep up to normal again as the new drug kicked in. Keeping the chart meant that I spent the minimum time possible without the help of a functioning anti-depressant.

The chart also allowed me to notice how logical every trough was, after I'd started to come out of the first, unremitting down. Combined with the diary I kept when I could, the chart showed that the lows weren't random glitches but were a response to overdoing things or trying to live 'normally' too soon. This is what I mean by listening to depression. I could even note when I'd slip off into obsessing again, because the evidence of the effect of such behaviour on my health was there, on paper, plain to see.

j) Dress better than you feel.

I used to have a grey fluffy cardigan that drove Leighton mad because he knew that I only ever wore it when I felt down. It was a good day when that cardigan finally left our house.

I had been brought up very much to believe that you kept your best clothes for being 'out in the world'. Depressives are known for wrapping themselves in colourless, unflattering clothes and generally looking as shapeless as a sausage without a skin.

When you're depressed your morale is so depleted that anything that lifts it should have top priority. You are the most important public you will ever have, so dress accordingly. Don't slop down to the post office with your pyjamas on under your trousers. Pick your favourite sweater and put on some lipstick. Why give the office all your best personal resources? Put on a suit to walk into town. Wax those legs, paint those nails! These seemingly trivial cosmetic matters have far-reaching psychological effects, and will do more for your recovery than you ever thought possible.

k) *Watch your diet.*

Of course, I'd rather eat potatoes than take anti-depressants, but I would never suggest substituting a diet for medication prescribed by a good doctor. I wish I could believe that eating no sugar and nothing but complex carbohydrates would stop me from becoming depressed, but while such a diet might be good for you, I'm too cravenly fond of treats to be able to give them up entirely.

I do, however, want to mention three points related to diet without being in the least faddy. I went through a major bout of clinical depression without missing one meal. (I think I might have missed one lunch, but I made up for it with cream crackers.) Regular meals are amazingly restorative to the morale, which can slip, with your blood sugar, without your noticing. Chocolate, however, has given me trouble in the past because it gives my mood a huge lift and then a corresponding down, leaving me craving for more. I mention this because more 'down' I do not need – not because I'm a puritan.

Alcohol, a depressant, is obviously not a good idea when you're down. For a similar reason, taking ecstasy is probably not a good idea. Whatever chemical adventures it offers, its effect on the brain chemistry can be sufficiently chaotic that my curiosity about its properties is now non-existent.

Our current understanding of brain chemistry is incomplete. All I know is that if there were endorphin mines, I'd go prospecting.

CHAPTER TWELVE

Burying the Dead

The problem with the dead is that they refuse to stay like that – unless you let them go.

The corpse I'm talking about here is you, the person you were before you became depressed. The only fortunate side effect of clinical depression's memory loss is that it helps you to forget your old, fake life, as you cross an internal Lethe on your way to the Underworld.

At first Jonathan Butlin might have thought he was being burgled on a daily basis by a minor thief. Then the realisation dawned that someone else was living in his house.

Sausages and eggs disappeared from the fridge, taken evidently by the same person who had been using the frying pan.

A £20 note was stolen, the shower had been used and the intruder drew the living room curtain halfway across to shield his eyes from the sun as he watched television.

After ten days of strange goings on Mr Butlin, 60, called the police and officers discovered an uninvited guest in the loft.

The squatter was Stephen Huggins, whom Mr Butlin had evicted from his home in Chester Street, Swindon, Wilts, three weeks previously because he owed rent.

The former tenant had returned, made himself comfortable in the attic and used the house as his own when Mr Butlin was out. Sean O'Neill, *Daily Telegraph*

Don't expect to recognise yourself when you recover. My taste in food has changed, and so has my skin. My old perfume smells sour on me, and I'm still looking for a replacement fragrance for my new life.

First of all, colour returned. I dreamt that I saw a huge, exotic bird in the sky. I snatched the binoculars from Leighton and watched a heron land near us. Its grey feathers were deceptively dull and had all kinds of iridescent colours in

them, peacock blues, opalescent greens, turquoises and tan-
gerines. And while we watched its plumage in wonder, the
heron spoke to us, making promises. I gorged on being able
to feel pleasure again. I even took to going to the cinema in
the afternoons on my own. I watched *A Bug's Life* in a
multiplex: me and one other person in the rhythmic, multi-
coloured dark.

Normally I hate going into town, but one day I *had*
to have make-up. Even though I usually run a mile from
the assistants, I let the Esteé Lauder girl help me select a lipstick. Looking at my clothes, the girl made a swift judgement and started showing me colours from the Natural
and Classic ranges. 'No, no,' I said, 'I need something
brighter.' Soon, I had moved through Rich and into Vivid. I
settled eventually on a startling fuchsia pink called All-Day
Island Kiss – a neon pink that almost glows in the dark. That
day there was no point to lipstick if it didn't shout. Then I
bought so many pots of nail varnish that they gave me two
free travel hairdryers. Recovery can be heavy on the credit
card.

Another time I went into town on my own 'just for a
look.' The only thing we really needed was a pint of milk. I
came home four hours later with a furry hat and a sparkling
black evening dress split to the hip. Of course, I forgot the
milk.

*

[Fernande Picasso] had the true french feeling about
a hat, if a hat did not provoke some witticism from
a man on the street the hat was not a success ...
She had on a large yellow hat and I had on a much
smaller blue one. As we were walking along a work-
man stopped and called out, there go the sun and
the moon shining together. Ah, said Fernande to me
with a radiant smile, you see our hats are a success.

Gertrude Stein, The Autobiography of Alice B. Toklas
(Penguin, 1966), p. 19

When you're depressed, it feels as though there is a huge
distance between you and things, which are inert, unrespon-
sive to your wishes. Now that I was feeling better, a pen
would leap into my hand, soap seemed to cover me of its
own accord, the towel would be in exactly the right place for
me to pick it up. Instead of being the slave of the objects
around me, I was part again of an active world in which I
could participate.

Now I looked around me and was ravished by continual
motion. Left sitting in the car while Leighton went for a
paper, I watched as, simultaneously, builders unloaded their
van, a dog wandered around the corner and a woman in an
overall went on an errand to the shops. Instead of the painful
jumping cuts of debilitation, now I was seeing the movies in
technicolour and I couldn't get enough.

OFF-THE-SHOULDER GOWN FOR
CRIBYN BRIDE

Headline, *Cambrian News*, 1983

When I first started to feel really well again, I became so excited that I couldn't sleep. Even though my energy was coming back, the current was unpredictable. I was suffering from domestic jet lag and my body was having difficulty in establishing its own time zone, because I'd slept so much.

I was coming home at last after having been away for a very long time. On the first night this happened, Leighton and I had tea and cake in bed at 4 am, to celebrate my return.

The grim part of depression's work was now over. The next task was to build the new life towards which my illness had pointed me. I'd done my homework, now it was time for the test.

I do know, that I was born
　　　To age, misfortune, sickness, grief:
But I will bear these, with that scorn,
　　　As shall not need thy false relief.
Nor for my peace will I go far,

As wanderers do, that still do roam,
But make my strengths, such as they are,
Here in my bosom, and at home.

Ben Jonson, 'To the World',
Ben Jonson: The Complete Poems,
ed George Parfitt (Penguin, 1980), pp. 102–3

Before I became ill, I'd been invited to give a reading in New York. The doctor certified me fit and Leighton came with me, to act as rottweiler and to make sure that I didn't overdo things.

On our first afternoon we went for a long walk in Central Park to blow away the plane's stale air. The outdoor skating rink was bathed in bright March sunlight. People were skating anti-clockwise to 'The Dying Swan' from *Swan Lake*. A lady with a purple coat and matching pom-poms on her skates was passed by an awkward boy in red who looked as though he was always just about to fall. Together they swirled slowly in a galaxy. On the fringes of the star system a class of teenage girls practised a disco routine, imitating their teacher, skating on one leg. A class of toddlers moved in a train, making a sawing action with their tiny feet. A supervisor skated expertly against the flow, shouting at youngsters who wanted to sabotage the large, gracious movement of the Milky Way.

This spectacle reduced me to tears. What moved me was

how vulnerable the skaters were and yet how they made an art out of their danger. Their individual body movements were in slow motion, but the ice took them far. Each skater, with their own way of taking care, of keeping going, was utterly individual, and yet the dignified spiral accommodated everybody – the elderly couples with a foxtrot grace and young men tearing around on testosterone.

And somehow, even though we watched a long time, that afternoon I didn't see anybody fall.

> When someone steps barefooted on a thorn,
> he immediately puts his foot on his knee and searches
> with a needle, and when he can't locate the tip,
> he moistens around the place with moisture
> from his lips. A splinter is often
> difficult to get out.
>   How much more difficult a thorn
> in the heart! If everyone could find that thorn
> in themselves, things would be
> much more peaceful here!

Rumi, The Essential Rumi, tr Coleman Barks
(HarperSanFrancisco, 1995), pp. 230–31

There's nothing like returning to a familiar place to make you notice how you've changed. Having pulled several thorns out of my heart since my time in New York, the city looked like a totally different place.

I thought that I knew every nook and cranny of the Metropolitan Museum of Art, but I found whole galleries of which I had no recollection. I'd had no interest in the Asian Galleries before but now found a wonderfully poised statue of a Zen master, humming with power in his glass case.

The real revelation, though, were the Egyptian galleries. Someone once said that 'psychoanalysis always happens in a museum.' As Leighton and I moved from case to case, we tried to reconstruct the race that had made separate coffins for a shrew, a crocodile and a beetle. We pieced together a ruined empire from the hieroglyphs and noted that even embalmed princes and queens couldn't live forever.

The curators were fighting a losing battle against flash. They possessed an authority entirely different from attendants in the American Wing because they were guarding the temple of the Kings of Upper and Lower Egypt.

'Yes,' I heard one attendant answer a visitor's question. 'You can walk down there to the Twentieth Century, through the Renaissance.'

This is a Lesson long enough: which you may be all your Life in Learning, and to all Eternity in Practising. *Be Sensible of your Wants, that you may be sensible of your Treasures.*

Thomas Traherne, *Poems, Centuries and Three Thanksgivings*, ed. Anne Ridler (OUP, 1966), The First Century, p. 184

It's a mistake to prefer museums to real life. The best exhibit of the day wasn't in the Egyptian Antiquities section, but just outside the building. As we were making our way to the Temple of Dendur in the Sackler Wing, I saw a tramp lying on the exterior windowsill of the museum, just where Central Park slopes down to the Met's tall glass walls.

It was cold but sunny. The man had taken his shirt off to sunbathe, and looked like one of the mummies with a funerary portrait wrapped around its head. His shirt was looped, like loosened bandages, around his arms. Behind him a stream of runners, taking part in a race, showed their Pharaonic profiles, as if they were illustrating this monarch's history.

I crept up to the glass and looked at him closely. The man had placed his shoes and socks neatly by his feet. I could see the creases in the skin underneath his breasts, and his chest rising and falling.

Whatever grandiose plans I'd had before, they were ruined, like the Egyptian trash stored in the glass cases. Here was the Egyptian wing's sovereign, resting simply in the sun, not thinking of empire, not even thinking.

*

Yet the live quarry all the same
Were changed to huntsmen in the game,
And the wild furies of the past,
Tracked to their origins at last.

W. H. Auden, 'New Year Letter',
op cit, p. 163

Later that afternoon, I gave myself over into the hands of the girls at Iris Nails to be embalmed for my reading. The Korean manicurists helped me choose the right colour to go with my kingfisher-blue suit. They made the rich girls of the Upper East Side who'd come for pedicures wear paper slippers, like slaves' sandals.

What I'd discovered during this depression was that everything I'd been afraid of simply wasn't true. I hadn't ruined anybody's life by pursuing my writing. Nor had poetry turned me into a monster. In fact, whenever I practised it with the right motives, it had become a powerful tool for discernment in my life. All the qualities I'd thought outside myself and in other people were already in my possession. If you admire something for long enough, you incorporate that virtue into yourself.

Even in the suffering of this last terrible depression, I had retained a sense of joy in living: I was not a younger version of my grandmother. I'd learned to ride out rough seas but had redeemed my past self-abandonments by proving self-constant. I also knew that depression, if I could bring myself not to hate it, could be a powerful force for wise change rather than the random chemical wipeout of personality I had always feared.

The nail-bar princesses chatted under a price-list cartouche while the Quick Nail Dryers whirred like scarab beetles. It took me a while to choose but, in the end, it came down to Saba Silver or gold. I went for the Montezuma Gold.

I already had everything I'd ever longed for.

> They had not gone far before they saw the Mock Turtle in the distance, sitting sad and lonely on a little ledge of rock, and, as they came nearer, Alice could hear him sighing as if his heart would break. She pitied him deeply. 'What is his sorrow?' she asked the Gryphon. And the Gryphon answered, very nearly in the same words as before, 'It's all his fancy, that: he hasn't got no sorrow, you know.'
>
> Lewis Carroll, *Alice's Adventures in Wonderland*,
> *The Complete Lewis Carroll*, Vol I, (Wordsworth Editions, 1999),
> pp. 92–3

*

The way forward for me lay in using a different part of myself to judge between true and false. The best way I can describe it is moving down from my head and into my stomach. The head is where all your fancies, recollections, gripes and projections are endlessly rehearsed. It's a Virtual Reality gallery dedicated to your personal preoccupations. Although the pictures are vivid – no, compelling – this area has no way of distinguishing between fantasy and truth, because both look just as convincing. The head, then, is very good at trying out possibilities, versions of reality, and totally unable to make moral choices between them.

The stomach doesn't work visually but viscerally. It 'sees' in the dark, but if listened to carefully, gives reliable guidance. It ties itself in knots when you're lying, and tells you what to do even before you have worked out why that should be right. Like a dog it is instinctive in its likes and dislikes and its decisions are invariably sound. The head tells you what could be, the stomach tells you what is.

When you're used to leading your life with your head, it's hard to move down and learn to see with another part of yourself. But the insights that come with the effort to do so are startling.

The only case of courage required of us: to be courageous in the face of the strangest, the most whimsical and unexplainable thing that we could encounter . . .

Only he who can expect anything, who does not exclude even the mysterious, will have a relationship with life greater than just being alive . . .

If we fashion our life according to that principle, which advises us to embrace that which is difficult, then that which appears to us to be the very strangest will become the most worthy of our trust, and the truest . . .

Perhaps all dragons in our lives are really princesses just waiting to see us just once being beautiful and courageous. Perhaps everything fearful is basically helplessness that seeks our help.

Rilke, *Letters to a Young Poet*, pp. 82–5

The wordlessness of depression is a galling experience. You can't phone your friends, writing an e-mail is beyond you, you can't put pen to paper. The disease is a crash-course in meaninglessness, lack of structure, the collapse of form.

Yet the human brain is amazingly adaptable. When neurological damage takes place, closing down the conventional paths of command and action, patients' nerve cells find new routes for communication. Recent research into sleep proposes the theory that dreams are internally generated stimuli which help the brain's neurons to grow and connect with one another and prevent the atrophy of the synapses during sleep. While all the normal activities of daily life are shut down, new creative connections are made in the subconscious.

When I first started talking again, strange things kept happening to my language. Often, I couldn't remember the usual word for an object, but would improvise, saying 'clicker' for 'indicator' or 'kettle' for 'cat'. These are tiny examples, but each modification did possess its own childish logic, and was a perfectly good circumlocution of the forgotten word. If new connections like these were being made at a vocabulary level, then even more important shifts must have been happening in the configuration of my ideas and values – a transformation which I couldn't yet begin to see.

Thus, on a literal level, I could see how depression was forcing my brain to be creative, to overcome its own deficiencies. For a poet, metre and rhyme work in much the same way. Because they're slightly different from the patterns of everyday speech, they push the brain to use unusual neural pathways. Thus, good poetry is always the enemy of cliché and conventional thought.

Metre and rhyme also offer a rationale of sorts while you're in the middle of finding out what on earth you might mean – a blind man's white stick, or the cats' eyes running up the middle of a road at night. They protect you as you explore painful memories, much as a skilled hypnotist keeps you calm as you're regressing to a stressful event. That way you're able to collect more evidence from the scene of the crime and to return into the present in safety.

This is not to say that an experience of depression is a compulsory vocational qualification for a writer. It's not. If you have it in your life, however, you might as well learn everything you can from it, because the price you and your family have paid for that knowledge is already extremely high.

> He made a list of experiences he thought he should have in order to become a better writer. He left No. 1 blank, for fear his mother might see it. No. 2 was Europe; No. 3 was despair.
>
> Garrison Keillor, *Lake Wobegon Days* (Faber, 1985) p. 462

Boredom is depression's younger cousin, a less virulent strain of the same overwhelming loss of meaning. I've learned, however, to see boredom as a crucial part of a writer's life. Like depression, boredom teaches you how fundamentally inadequate your own dull thoughts are, even to yourself. And if you're not interested in your own tedium, who else will be? Boredom pushes you out beyond your habitual thinking, makes you desperately creative, helps you to come up with something new.

Prophylactic doses of boredom and depression together in the form of meditation are very helpful in building up a resistance to them in your emotional immune system. After all, neither is fatal. Together they form the poverty of spirit which Christ promised would be comforted. They're not important in themselves but for the gifts they bring in their wake. Dark gifts, but lasting treasures.

> Some meditation should be boring, should be as boring as possible, because in intense boredom all our habitual responses and concepts are dissolved. The mind's terror of boredom is the more acute because the mind suspects that through boredom, through its extreme experience, another reality might be reached that would threaten its pretentions, and perhaps even dissolve them altogether.
>
> Andrew Harvey, *A Journey in Ladakh*, Picador, 1993, p. 184

In the first year of our marriage, Leighton and I sometimes had similar dreams. One night I dreamt that I was pregnant with twins. I was very concerned about enduring a long labour but Leighton was suddenly there and said, 'You silly bugger, look, I can see the head,' and reached into me and pulled out a baby boy covered in blood. When I told him my dream, the real Leighton told me that he'd dreamt that he was pulling a spear out of my arm.

The babies I dream about now aren't real ones. Depression has changed their meaning. I still dream from time to time that I'm pregnant, and have learned that this isn't a bad omen, but it is usually related to my writing. It's a sign that I'm about to start on a piece of work. It's not a reproach but a blessing on what I *can* do, and I always enjoy those pregnancies to the full.

Prince Korasoff to Julien Sorrel:

> 'Why, you look like a Trappist, you're overdoing the principle of gravity I gave you in London. A melancholy air can never be good form; what you want is to look bored. If you're melancholy, it means you want something you haven't got, or there's something in which you haven't succeeded. *That's an admission of inferiority.* On the other hand, if you're bored, it means that the person who has vainly tried to please you is your inferior. Realize, my dear fellow, what a grave mistake you are making.'

> Stendhal, *Scarlet and Black*, tr. Margaret R. B. Shaw
> (Penguin, 1979), p. 399

*

Recovering from this depression has forced me to put a new model of myself into practical action. In this new inner cosmology, there's no 'out there' for me. I should know, because I spent long enough running around looking for it. The qualities and resources on which I can rely are all here, now, even if I don't have faith in their ability to get me through. They're always enough, if I remember to rely on them.

When the Buddhists say that the ego is a fiction, I don't think they mean that the ego isn't there, but that it isn't real. It's only when you learn to live outside it – relying on the stomach as opposed to the head is another way of describing this – that the personality takes its proper place. The ego is useful as a role adopted by one part of the whole self, but it is no compass.

Simone Weil says that 'the only organ of contact with existence is acceptance, love'. She doesn't mean by this that we should regard life with mushy emotion, she's saying that awareness is a more accurate form of perception than analysis. She means that you can only see people accurately when you renounce the vested interest your ego might have in them, and see them for themselves. Being unselfish is important, therefore, not because it's virtuous but that way you gain the most reliable picture of reality. This has nothing to do with morals and everything to do with conforming to the truth of how energy and our constitutions work together.

The very best reason for doing something is because there's nothing in it for you. This is the important thing, whether we're talking about raising children, writing or any other great undertaking in life. This doesn't mean that you won't gain enormously from the experience of watching a child explore the world or training yourself to see beauty. The important thing is that when your gain isn't the primary reason for doing something, then you're less likely to mess it up with your egotism.

> The intellect is less strict than the spirit. The spirit, which is the final judge, does not exhaust us with arguments, it simply forces us to look.
>
> Alain, *The Gods*, tr Richard Pevear
> (Quartet Books, 1988), p. 154

After so many months depressed, with nothing much happening, when my life changed, it happened all in a rush.

It was as if my illness had allowed me to pull myself into new focus. Suddenly I knew that I had to change my job or become ill again, so I applied for a post in the arts world. As part of the research for my interview I was invited to take part in a mixed-ability drama class run by the Hijinx Theatre Company, which included people with learning disabilities. I enjoyed the warm-up exercises because none of them made me feel foolish. Then something startling happened.

There's an exercise called the 'Yes/ No Game' which requires two people to act out a whole scene together using only those two words. I was partnered with another Gwyneth, a blonde, mischievous woman with Down's Syndrome. We didn't plan our scene beforehand. I sat in a chair with my head in my hands and groaned 'No. No! Noooo!', as if in despair. Gwyneth stood to my right and countered my Nos with a repeated 'Yes!', patiently coaxing me out of my misery.

Slowly I raised my head and asked, 'No?' Gwyneth came closer and closer, whispering her Yeses until her mouth was next to my ear. Then, when we were finally face to face, she rubbed her nose against mine and said, 'Give me a kiss!' and we (and our audience) collapsed laughing.

That night I dreamt of Gwyneth's blonde face, close and huge in front of mine, filling my vision, and she was golden and full of joy.

That weekend I withdrew my application for the job and decided that I'd become a freelance writer. Before my depression I wouldn't have dared take such a step, but suffering makes you fearless. A year later, I went to a Hijinx performance and found Gwyneth backstage. I thanked her and gave her a badge with our name on it. She was delighted and put it on straight away. I'd found my doppelgänger, my unlikely twin.

*

Since that day, I hardly recognise my life. Once things started moving, they gushed, like a river roaring out of underground caverns into daylight.

Within a month, I'd taken voluntary redundancy and, almost by accident, Leighton had acquired a yellow boat. When we had tried sailing in the past, I'd been so seasick that I'd sworn never to set foot on a boat again. Now, however, my body seemed to have changed and I was less debilitated – perhaps I'd acquired my sea legs by enduring depression's vertigo for so long. Seasickness, by the way, is the nearest external equivalent I know to depression. You feel nauseous, disorientated and you couldn't care less about anything.

Six months later, we had bought a thirty-five foot Nicholson, a yacht big enough to take us round the globe and we were planning our trip. We found *Jameeleh* in the Beaulieu River and had her brought to Cardiff by road. Her arrival excited a good deal of interest and admiration at Penarth marina: 'Look! She's even got teak decks!' Dougie, the driver, took off the clamps before *Jameeleh* was lifted off the lorry and into the water. The braces were covered in carpet. 'Bedroom quality!' Dougie winked.

I stood to one side, watching the process of unloading and lowering the boat. Leighton told me later that my head didn't move, only my eyes, and that my mouth was a big round O.

If I hadn't been depressed and learnt so much from it, I would never have had the courage to go sailing, let alone to spend all my redundancy money on a boat. Now going away to sea, a childhood dream of mine, is becoming a reality. We've already qualified as Day Skippers in navigation and

Leighton, who's remembering everything he knew in the merchant navy, can't sleep at night because he's so excited. This totally unexpected and unlikely prospect has come directly out of being depressed.

When you're in the middle of your depression, pay good attention to it, because, tended carefully, you never know where it might lead you.

My favourite exhibit in the National Museum of Wales in Cardiff is a Japanese plate which has obviously been broken and repaired. The masters of the Japanese tea ceremony used deliberately to drop precious dishes, in order that they might be rebuilt and, thus, be more beautiful than the original.

Used properly, depression is a breaking of the self that can lead to an even better healing. My Japanese porcelain has been repaired with gold, which streaks like lighting across the shattered plate.

I wouldn't swap my life now for anything.

ACKNOWLEDGEMENTS

The author and publishers are grateful to the proprietors listed below for permission to quote the following material:

Extract from *Life: A User's Manual* by Georges Perec © Hachette 1970, English translation by David Bellos © David Bellos 1987. Reproduced by permission of the Harvill Press. Extract from *The Times Atlas & Encyclopaedia of the Sea* by Alastair Couper © Alastair Couper 1989. Reproduced by permission of HarperCollins Publishers. Extract from *Humboldt's Gift* by Saul Bellow published by Secker & Warburg. Used by permission of the Random House Group Ltd. Extract from *Zen And The Art of Motorcycle Maintenance* by Robet Pirsig, published by Bodley Head. Used by permission of the Random House Group Limited. Extract from *The Holiday* by Stevie Smith, published by Virago, 1986. Used by permission of James McGibbon. Extract from 'Heavy Date' and 'New Year Letter' taken from *Collected Poems* by W.H. Auden. Used by permission of Faber and Faber Ltd. Extract from *Zen Mind, Beginner's Mind* by Shunryu Suzuki. Used by permission of Weatherhill Publishers. Extract from *The Heart of the Enlightened* by Anthony de Mello © Fount 1989. Used by permission of the Random House Group Limited. Teilhard de Chardin extract taken from *The Tao of Jesus*, ed Loya, Ho and Jih, 1998. Used by permission of The Paulist Press.

We have made every reasonable effort to trace all copyright-holders of quoted material, apologise for any omissions and are happy to receive emendations from copyright-holders.

P.S.

Ideas,
interviews
& features . . .

Getting Out of the Cave

Gwyneth Lewis talks to Louise Tucker

How did you know when you were ready, when it was no longer dangerous to write the book?

I think I wrote it before it was really safe to do so. But it was a trade-off between still being able to remember what being seriously depressed was like, which disappears once you're better, and not wanting to go back into that terrain. It wasn't without cost. People ask me quite often, 'Did you find writing the book cathartic?' and I say, 'Well, no, I'd done my therapy.' The difference the book made was it showed me the extent to which we're not alone when we're depressed because so many people came up to me afterwards and confessed or confided their own histories or those of their family and friends. This has changed forever the way I view depression because it is so much more prevalent than I thought. But I wouldn't recommend writing a book about depression as a cure for it because it's not.

How long did it take you?

I wrote it really quickly, in four months. But I knew I had a limited window of opportunity, because I only had a certain amount of courage to look at the deep past so I had to work fast. I couldn't write the book now. This is why it's so important to take your depression seriously because the roots it gives you down into your own life, to your past, change and possibilities disappear unless you grasp the opportunity to explore things while you can.

What was the overwhelming sense when you finished?

Relief. And wanting to move on. I was ready to do so because the writing of the book dovetailed very well with starting to sail. It was as if giving an account of my depression left me free to go sailing. It all happened in that sequence.

What inspired you to use the theme of detection?

You have to commit to a search and a detective is not going to let go. There is a real sense of unravelling a mystery since if there weren't something unknown at the heart of these matters why would we have such difficulty with them? You have to unravel what other people have told you about yourself because you tend to believe them and it's not always true. Especially if they're adults and you're a child. I think in some ways it's easier to accept other people's descriptions of yourself than to formulate your own. It's painful to find out the real thing but if you're depressed you have no choice because other people's versions have already not worked for you. So the detective is the last resort; if you don't discover your real self, then you're not going to get out of trouble.

'Self-help is the last thing a depressive needs.' As someone who has experienced the full range of depressive illness, what can self-help do?

I love self-help books, I've learnt an ▶

❛Sunbathing in the Rain showed me the extent to which we're not alone when we're depressed because so many people came up to me afterwards and confessed or confided their own histories or those of their family and friends.❜

3

Author photo © David Hurn

LIFE
at a Glance

I was born in Cardiff, to a Welsh-speaking family. After college, I spent three years in the US. I then worked in television before going freelance as a writer. I live in Cardiff with my husband.

Getting Out of the Cave *(continued)*

◄ enormous amount from them over the years, but I think it's a question of what you need at any given point. If you're in the middle of a depressive episode you're beyond self-help, because what you've been doing has got you into that mess. In my case I was completely shattered, exhausted and living by quite outmoded ideas about my own emotional life. What I needed to do was ditch those ideas and having serious depression did that for me.

'Regular outings, food, comfort' are the things that you sought out in recovery, very simple things that you, and many others, find hard to give themselves. How do you manage your needs now?
I struggle with this all the time. The most important things in life are the easiest to forget yet the simplest to achieve, and they are the first things that go by the board when you're feeling low. Going out for a walk every day without fail is excellent but it seems impossible to do if you're feeling down. I think our minds are often elsewhere, on thinking, as opposed to basic things like eating well, exercising, being kind to yourself. Anybody, unless you're severely debilitated, can go out for a twenty-minute walk. You don't have to run a marathon and, in fact, I fully intend never to run a marathon.

'Judging is irrelevant to living.' In a certain sense too much judgement causes depression yet we are asked to do this every day. How did you step out of it?
Once you let your mind go into that whole

dialogue of 'Am I doing well? Am I doing badly?' you're onto a loser because it doesn't matter at all how you're doing in life, as long as you're alive and living well.

It's quite a radical thing to live without external judgement, but it's also one of those things that make life worth living, those moments when we manage it. All the things I enjoy most have nothing to do with 'doing well'. Sometimes they're to do with 'doing badly'. I run badly, but I don't care, I love it and there's no relationship between doing it well and how important it is in my life. I think all depressives are savage about themselves. It's a liability and a very serious one.

Do you have a sense now of when you're well and can you appreciate it? Is it very much more balanced for you now, watching the triggers, respecting the triggers?
Overall, I am hugely more stable than I was but, having said that, depression still takes me by surprise. The first thing I notice is that I can't deal with emails any more because they take more expressive energy than I've got; I stay up late watching television; I can't get up in the morning. And my big one is going into overdrive: I know I might crash soon so anything that needs to be done, has to be done quickly.

What do you do when you see those triggers?
I readjust priorities, so I'll cut back on what I do so that I'm not exhausted, try and take some exercise, eat better and just be aware that it's happening. That's usually enough. If I'm feeling really bad, I've got emotional ▶

❝I wrote the book really quickly, in four months. But I knew I had a limited window of opportunity, because I only had a certain amount of courage to look at the deep past so I had to work fast. I couldn't write the book now.❞

5

Getting Out of the Cave *(continued)*

◄ support structures that I turn to. I go and see my psychiatrist. I don't go regularly any more but we keep in touch. I might go every two months or so and we review my situation and whether or not I should go back on the medication. At the moment I'm not on any medication as I'm doing very well without it. I don't live in terror of depression but I keep a wary eye on it.

Is recovery something organic, that you let happen?
Yes and no. I think as you come out of a serious episode, there are places, junctions at which you can decide whether to go back into it. Dorothy Rowe is very good on this: you can go back into this kind of cave if you like. It's quite scary to choose not to because you have to face everything that you're afraid of. I think that I have such a healthy fear of depression that I would do anything rather than go back there but, for me, it is a continual choice. This isn't true, though, for all types of the disease.

In terms of recovery, are there any lessons that can be applied to other people or do you think it's a very personal thing?
No, I think there are some basics which can help, which is why I want to pass them on. There is a way of reacting to difficult situations which doesn't lead to you shutting down and triggering the depression.

By shutting down I mean going back to bed, pulling the duvet over your head, isolating yourself from people. In order to get the energy to keep out of that cavern you

6 The most important things in life are the easiest to forget yet the simplest to achieve, and they are the first things that go by the board when you're feeling low. 9

have to venture out towards other people. That's where you get the new energy from, not from yourself and certainly not from staying in the dark . . . so let's get out of the cave. ∎

Gwyneth Lewis's Favourite Books about Depression

The Little Book of Beating the Blues
Cheri Huber
This is brilliant, my favourite book ever on depression. It has line drawings and lots of common sense in unexpected directions.

Nature Cure
Richard Mabey

Depression: The Way Out of Your Prison
Dorothy Rowe

Harry Potter and the Prisoner of Azkaban
J.K. Rowling
For the Dementors and because it's important to educate young people about depression. It's frightening unless you understand it.

Malignant Sadness
Lewis Wolpert

An Unquiet Mind: A Memoir of Moods and Madness
Kay Redfield Jamison
An account of bipolar depression.

A Mood Apart: A Thinker's Guide to Emotion and its Disorders
Peter C. Whybrow

The Noonday Demon: An Anatomy of Depression
Andrew Solomon

Women Who Run with the Wolves: Contacting the Power of the Wild Woman
Clarissa Pinkola Estés
Using fairy stories as directions for staying creatively healthy.

Awareness
Anthony de Mello
Not about depression, but has great stuff about the self.

The Zen Path Through Depression
Philip Martin ■

The Dos and Don'ts of Depression

by Gwyneth Lewis

Don't:

- attempt the *Bible*, *War and Peace* or *A la recherche du temps perdu*
- join a gym for the first time in fifteen years
- push yourself to do anything
- make any decisions while you're depressed
- forget that all that goes up must come down
- tolerate people who pull you down
- even think about how you are every day
- compare yourself with anyone else
- wish your depression away
- let depression stop you from enjoying yourself

❝Disentangle the "given facts" of your life (things you can't change) from the choices you've made in your reactions to these facts (things you can change).❞

❝What really hurts is your own self-abandonment: once you've started the process, you can hardly blame other people for following your lead.❞

Do:

- remember that depression can't harm you, only your reaction to it
- remember that depression always ends
- listen to what depression is telling you, and change your life accordingly
- remember that however much you blame other people, depression will only take you back to yourself
- learn how to distinguish between your rubbish and what's true
- dress better than you feel
- watch your diet
- pace yourself
- let go of what things mean
- look at *how* you're doing things, as well as *what* you're doing

‘Cognitive therapists focus on getting patients to see the glass as half full rather than half empty ... A more radical tactic would be to abolish the need for evaluation at all and just accept the glass as it is, whether it be cracked or brimming.’

Internal Meteorology

by Gwyneth Lewis

AFTER I'D BEEN at home from work for six months or so in 1999, suffering from a moderately serious bout of clinical depression, colleagues who knew I was a writer would ask me 'And are you writing?' I'd gasp and then explain that I couldn't even lift a fountain pen, get dressed or read a newspaper. How was I going to fashion highly structured poems, when I couldn't even remember if I'd washed myself or not in the last half-hour? People who are not obsessed by writing, as I am, seem to think that it's an activity that can be fitted in while you're watching television. I think that my colleagues' well-meaning question was informed by a further misconception, namely that a writer needs to be unhappy in order to create work. Wrong. A writer needs to have an overflow of morale and possibly misplaced confidence in his or her abilities to produce anything. Depression, with its crushing deficit of joie de vivre is writing's enemy. Or is it?

The statistics about the incidence of mental illness among writers are very striking. Poets and artists are far more likely to suffer from depression and to kill themselves than the rest of the population. It's tempting to deduce from this that depression might be helpful to an artist. But just because polar bears and melting icebergs are found in the same place doesn't mean that the polar bears are responsible for global warming. Having thought a great deal about the connections between creativity and depression, I think that the relationship between the two might be quite different from how it looks at first sight.

However instinctive a writer you are, there are always voices outside (from family members or friends who have a vested interest in keeping you as a conformist, part of a group) trying to dissuade you from saying the most individualistic, true and often uncomfortable things about your life. These later become internalized and can cripple you creatively. They are the writer's main enemy.

After many months of being Depressed Woman in a Dressing Gown, and with the unstinting help of Leighton, who fed me, allowed me to be ill and then encouraged me to start living again, I felt the need of a book that could place the horrible fog of depression in some kind of perspective. My concentration was still shot to pieces, and I couldn't read anything too long or heavy. The existing books I found about depression were . . . depressing. So I decided to write my own, while I could still remember exactly the bleakness of that emotional desert. So, I started to write *Sunbathing*.

Slowly, I began to see that, far from being an enemy, depression might be an unwelcome but, ultimately, kind friend. By pulling the plug on all the activities which were making me ill, it allowed me a safe breathing space to reconstruct a less punishing and more sustainable creative life. Depression might be a sign not that ▶

6 Having thought a great deal about the connections between creativity and depression, I think that the relationship between the two might be quite different from how it looks at first sight. 9

Internal Meteorology *(continued)*

◀ you're doing something wrong, but that you're doing something very right by stopping, reassessing and developing new values in your life. Not that I'd want it to come and live with me permanently. It's like a difficult relative. Fine to have in for a cup of tea but make sure that she leaves the premises.

Writing this book wasn't cathartic for me because I'd already done my therapy work, but it was helpful to have the whole experience written down, and physically away from me. Hearing other people's response to the book has become increasingly important to me. As a further part of recovery Leighton and I began to learn to sail. In weather patterns I could see the emotional depression that had floored me in atmospheric terms and this extended my understanding of the metaphor. For example, high pressure systems sound stressful, but because no air is able to move, they are very stable, with no wind. Low pressure, however, leads to storms because wind flows in to replace rising air, creating the familiar warm and cold fronts. This explains the emotional turbulence which can be created by an unstable internal meteorology.

And this is, perhaps, where the true relationship between creativity and depression lies. Dylan Thomas described writing poetry as walking through broken glass on your eyeballs. Far from being delicate, sensitive creatures poets are, when you consider the nature of their work, a kind of SAS of the spirit. When you write creatively, you take a chance on failing utterly;

6 When you write creatively, you take a chance on failing utterly. Far from being wimps, poets are prone to depression because they spend far more time in this terrain of ambiguity than the rest of the population who will do anything rather than face the existential blank wall that is the only gateway to worthwhile creative work. 9

you face your own incoherence in a brutal way; you live with not knowing what to do, how things will work out; indeed, only by weaving this into your work can you begin to construct a set of words that make sense. Poems require a daily input of incomplete knowledge. Far from being wimps, poets are prone to depression because they spend far more time in this terrain of ambiguity than the rest of the population who will do anything (get drunk, get laid, watch football, go on holiday) rather than face the existential blank wall that is the only gateway to worthwhile creative work.

So, to go back to my colleagues' question, no, I wasn't writing when I was actually depressed, but I've done a lot since. Partly because I'm now less frightened of things not making sense and I have a deep trust in meaning taking place in us subconsciously, whatever the 'thinky' part of the brain is up to. And writing, after all, has to be unafraid of the dark, and you can sunbathe in the shadows as well.

A version of this article previously appeared in *Mslexia* (www.mslexia.co.uk). ■

If You Loved This,
You Might Like ...

On Surviving Disaster

The Shipping News
Annie Proulx
The story of the fundamental transformation
of Quoyle from unloved, unemployed
widower, into a man with purpose and love.
That might sound like an overweening
parable but it's not: this is one of the best
uplifting novels ever, with not a trace of the
happy-clappy or moralizing.

On Creativity

The Artist's Way
Julia Cameron
A practical guide to paying more attention
to creativity. A classic self-help book.

Becoming a Writer
Dorothea Brande
Don't bother with any other books about
writing until you've read this one.

On Recovering from Depression

As Gwyneth Lewis makes clear, reading is
not something that the severely depressed
tend to manage. However, at the recovery
stage there are many books that are highly
recommended such as these two.

Overcoming Depression
Paul Gilbert
A cognitive behavioural approach, so best for
those who are in recovery.

Breaking the Bonds: Understanding Depression, Finding Freedom
Dorothy Rowe
Dorothy Rowe's books are clear, realistic and very accessible.

On Living Well

Authentic Happiness
Martin E.P. Seligman
Seligman was the originator of positive psychology, the search for why we feel good (as opposed to the therapeutic focus since Freud on why we feel bad) and his practical book on the subject is highly regarded.

Families and How to Survive Them
John Cleese and Robin Skynner
A classic and deservedly so. Cleese's name might make you think this is a parody but it's far from it. It's written in the style of a conversation with his family therapist which makes it more approachable than many other books. Their second book *Life and How to Survive It*, about how to establish good mental health, is also very readable. ∎

HAVE YOU READ?

Other non-fiction by Gwyneth Lewis

Two in a Boat
When Gwyneth Lewis sets off to sail round the world with husband Leighton and a yacht named *Jameeleh*, she has no concept that the journey that awaits her has nothing to do with the oceans. As disaster follows disaster, and Leighton turns into 'Captain Bastard', a whole other adventure unfolds, one that threatens the happily ever after she hoped for but which takes the couple into rich uncharted waters.

Find Out More

Searching on the internet for depression throws up many selections, but sadly a lot of the resources available are unsuitable for anyone suffering or recovering from depression, because they are too academic, too complicated or not user-friendly (e.g. tiny fonts used, too many choices offered, lots of irrelevant information provided). This is a selection of the most helpful in the UK.

www.depression.org.uk
This 'Defeating Depression' website, initiated by the Sir Robert Mond Memorial Trust, a mental health charity registered in the UK, offers very thorough but accessible resources, practical information and links to organizations across the world that can help. The organizations search is broken down into different types (counselling, anxiety, eating disorders amongst others) and parts of the world. A practical guide aimed at those who are well enough to start moving forward, or their carers, can be downloaded at **www.defeatdepression.org/pdf/patientguide2.pdf**. Unlike a lot of sites this one is concise and easy to navigate.

www.samaritans.org.uk
Confidential free emotional support for the distressed, depressed and suicidal available 24 hours a day in the UK. Counsellors can be contacted by phone, email, text or in person.

www.mind.org.uk
Mind is the most well-known mental health charity in the UK. The information pages offer limited factsheets and 'making sense' sections.